Waldemar Góralski

The Japanese Aircraft Carrier Shinano

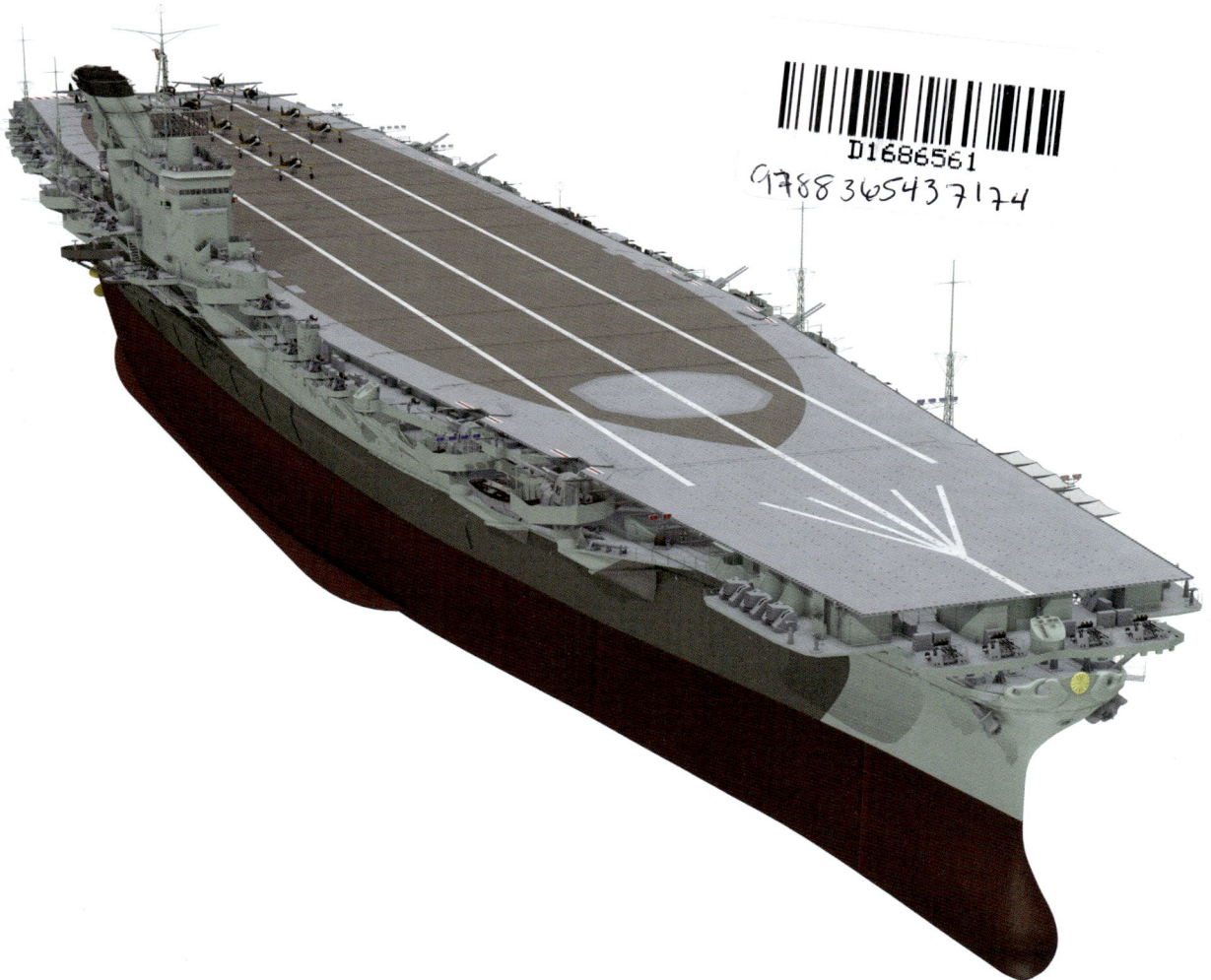

Ladies and Gentlemen

I invite you on a virtual walk around a ship which did not achieve anything, but became a legend anyway. I based the construction of the model of *Shinano* on materials, which are rather scarce. Only one wartime photograph, a few drawings and not particularly detailed plans survived. Some models of *Shinano* were also released and I used them as a point of reference to my model. The model of *Shinano* presented in this book is my vision and details of the decks are analogous to other Japanese World War Two warships. So could this ship look in 1944. I express thanks to Wojciech Niewęgłowski (Kliment) for rendering carrier based aircraft for this publication.

KAGERO publishing

View of *Shinano's* port side.

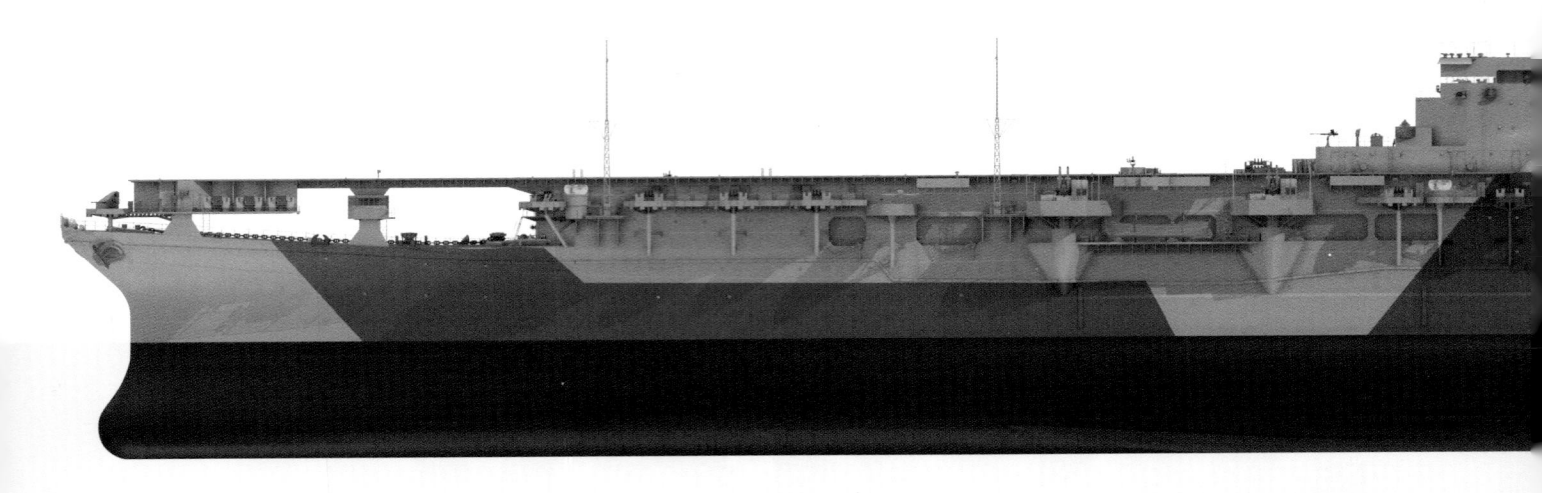

On 4 May 1940 the third Yamato-class battleship was laid down at the Navy Shipyard in Yokosuka. It was to be named *Shinano*, after a province on the Honshu island, in Nagato prefecture. That was also the name of the longest river in Japan (320 km). Admiral Yamamoto was born at its banks. Due to material supply difficulties, in December 1940 the construction was suspended. In 1942, after Japanese defeat at Midway (four aircraft carriers were lost) it was decided to continue the construction of the ship as an aircraft carrier, in order to partially make up for losses suffered in this class of ships. The rebuilding scheme was designed by Vice Admirals Keji Fukuda and Seichi Izamura. The hull was almost complete, so there were no interferences in the size and displacement. In place of the barbettes of the main artillery and part of armor aviation fuel tanks of capacity of 720,000 liters were installed. The tanks were armored with steel plates and layer of concrete. In the hull magazines of ammunition and spare parts for aircraft were built. Apart from participation in combat operations *Shinano* was to serve as logistic center for smaller carriers. On the deck a single-store hangar, 153,4 m long and 33,8 m wide was built. The hangar had two elevators, one on the bow and stern each. The hangar could house up to 120 aircraft. The carrier air group consisted of up to 50 aircraft, the remaining aircraft were intended as replacement for other carriers. The hangar was divided by fire curtain. The rear part was intended for the carrier air group, and the remaining two-thirds were intended for overhauls and storage of remaining aircraft. The ventilation devices and their outlets were, for the first time on a carrier, armored with 37-mm plates.

The propulsion and other systems were the same as on previous Yamato-class vessels. The ship was powered by four Kampon geared turbines rated at 150,000 shp (110,000 kW) in total. The steam for turbines was generated by 12 Kampon Ro-Go boilers at pressure of 25 kg/cm² and temperature of 352 degrees Celsius. The ship was propelled by four propellers.

The hull's armor was 160 – 230 mm thick, the decks were 100 – 190 mm thick. The flight deck was armored with 76 mm thick plates and could withstand the explosion of a 500 kg bomb (the largest one carried by US carrier-based aircraft).

The main armament of the ship comprised sixteen 127 mm guns on 89 A1 twin mounts. They had the maximum horizontal firing range 14,700 m and vertical 9,440 m. The maximum elevation angle was 90 degrees and the rate of fire was 14 rounds per minute.

Light anti-aircraft weaponry consisted of 145 (35 triple-mounted and 40 single) 25 mm Type 96 cannons. The effective range was 1,500

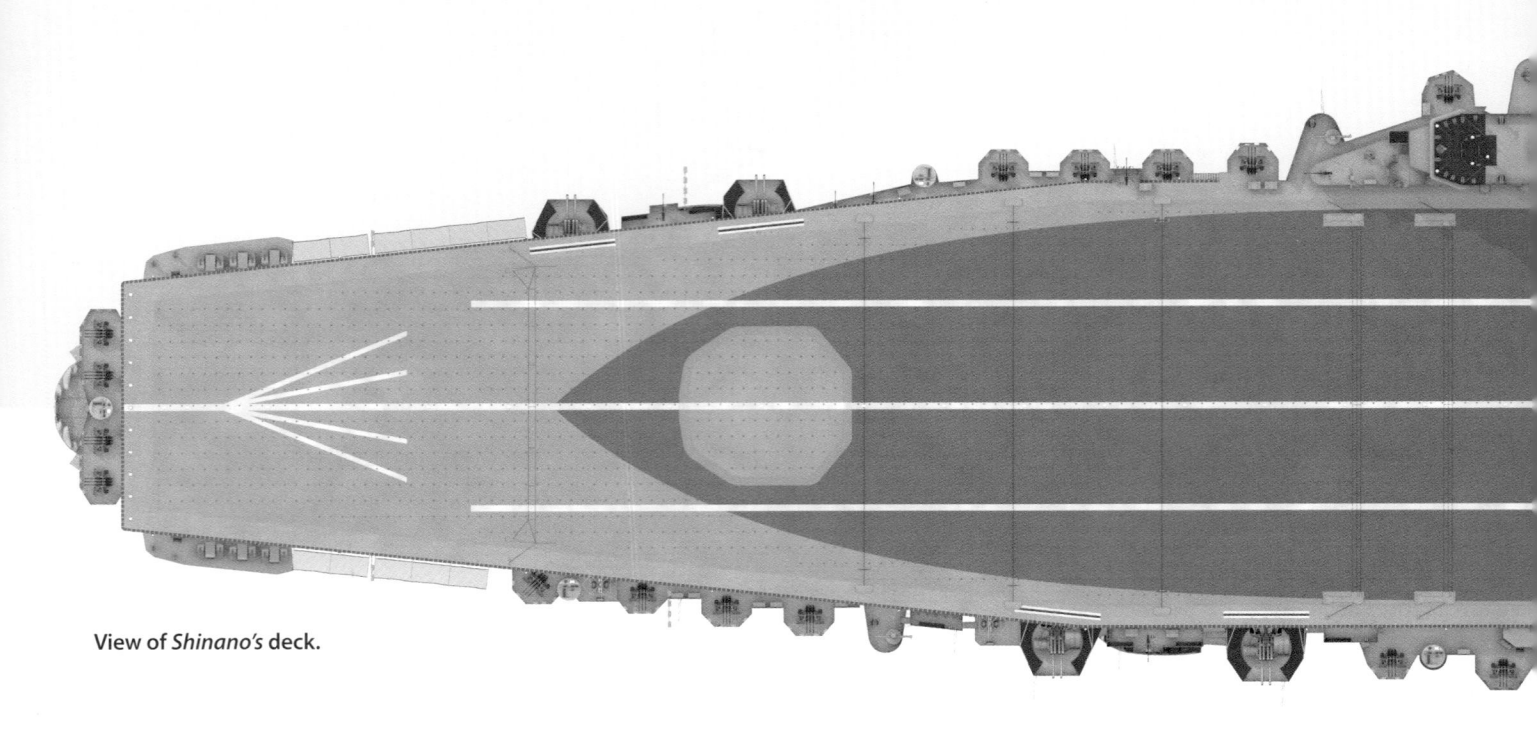

View of *Shinano's* deck.

– 3,000 m. The maximum elevation angle was 85 degrees and the rate of fire was 110 – 160 rounds per minute.

Apart from the artillery the ship had also 12 packages of 120 mm unguided rockets, with 28 launchers in each package. The rocket's weight was 22.5 kg, the velocity was 200 m/s and the range was 4,800 m.

For fire control of 127 mm guns four Type 94 gun directors, one per each pair of guns were used. Type 13 and 22 radars were also installed. The ship was equipped with 4.5 m rangefinder and three 90-cm searchlights.

The carrier air group of *Shinano* was to consist of 20 (two spare) Mitsubishi A7M Reppu (Sam) fighters, 20 (two spare) Aichi B7A Ryusei (Grace) torpedo-dive bombers and seven (one spare) Nakajima C6N Saiun (Myrt) reconnaissance aircraft.

On 5 October 1944, during the floating-out procedure the forward hydrophones were damaged.

On 8 October *Shinano* was launched and on 11 November underwent sea trials in the Gulf of Kisarazu. On 19 November the ship was commissioned by Imperial Japanese Navy and Captain Toshio Abe was appointed the ship's commander.

On 28 November *Shinano* departed Yokosuka for Kure Naval Arsenal for fitting-out, watertight doors were to be installed among others. A group of shipyard workers, doing the finishing work was aboard. The ship carried 50 MXY7 Ohka suicide flying bombs with crews and six Shinyo suicide boats. The escort during the passage consisted of the destroyers Yukikaze, Isokaze and Hamakaze. On 29 November the group

Specifications

Shipyard	Yokosuka Navy Shipyard
Laid down	4 May 1940
Launched	8 October 1944
Commissioned	19 November 1944
Displacement	standard: 65,800 ts full: 69,151 ts
Length	265.8 m
Beam	36.3 m
Draught	10.28 m (max 11.67 m)
Flight deck	256 x 40 m
Propulsion	12 Kampon boilers, four Kampon geared turbines rated at 150,000 shp, four propellers
Maximum speed	27 kt.
Range	7,200 NM at 16 kt.
Armament	16 x 127 mm (8x2) 145 x 25 mm (35x3, 40x1) 336 x 120 mm rocket launchers (12x28)
Carrier air group	20 (18+2) Mitsubishi A7M Reppu fighters, 20 (18+2) Aichi B7A Ryusei (Grace) torpedo-dive bombers, 7(6+1) Nakajima C6N Saiun (Myrt) reconnaissance aircraft
Complement	2,400 officers and men

Starboard side of the carrier.

Front view.

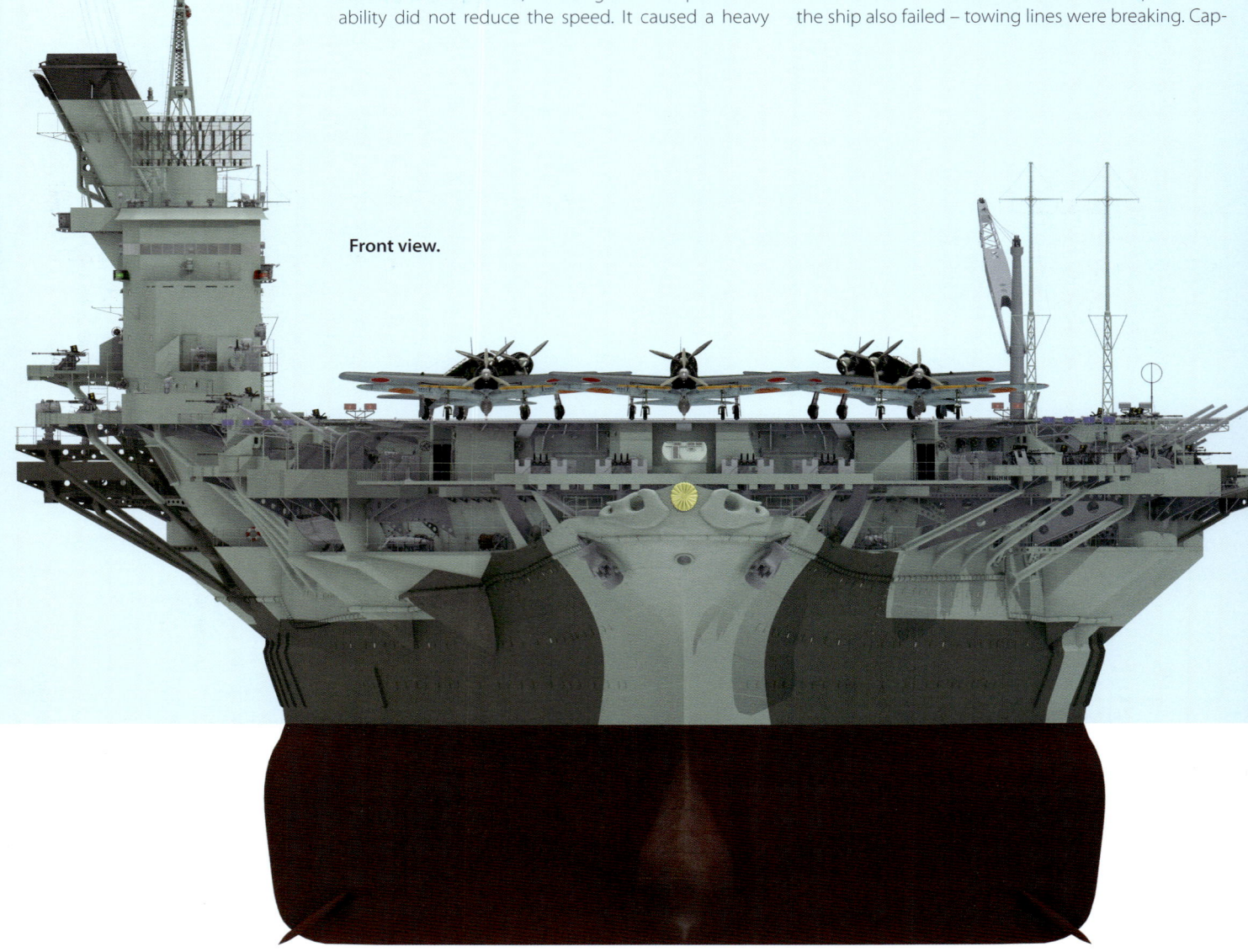

was spotted by American submarine USS Archerfish (SS-311), commanded by Cdr Enright south of Honshu. The submarine was sent to that area to search for a downed B-29 bomber crew. After a short chase Archerfish launched a salvo of six torpedoes at *Shinano*. Four of them hit the target – three in the starboard side amidships and one near the stern. After the hits Toshio Abe, believing in the ship's unsinkability did not reduce the speed. It caused a heavy ingress of water into the hull, resulting in a list to starboard side. The crew tried to level the ship, flooding the port side caissons, but it did not help. The list was increasing. Lack of watertight doors and unsealed holes in bulkheads, through which several cables and pipes ran hampered to control the flood. Panic of civilian workers and the crew's lack of training in rescue actions had their effect too. Attempts to tow the ship also failed – towing lines were breaking. Captain Abe ordered the crew to abandon the ship. The destroyer Yukikaze approached and took a part of the crew on board. At 1057 hours *Shinano* capsized and sank at coordinates: 32°07'N 137°04'E near the island of Jnamba. Captain Toshio Abe along with 1,435 crewmembers and shipyard workers went down with the ship. Rescued were 1,080 men (55 officers, 993 enlisted men and petty officers, 32 shipyard workers and three suicide pilots). The survivors were isolated on the island of Mitsuko-jima in the Gulf of Kure until January 1945.

Initially nobody believed Commander Enright's claim to have sunk an aircraft carrier. When he submitted a drawing of the ship, it was classified as Hayatake-class aircraft carrier. Only after the war the Americans learned about the sinking of *Shinano*. For this feat Commander Joseph F. Enright was awarded the Navy Cross.

Wiśniewski Piotr

Rear view.

The Japanese Aircraft Carrier Shinano

Bow of *Shinano* seen from the port side.

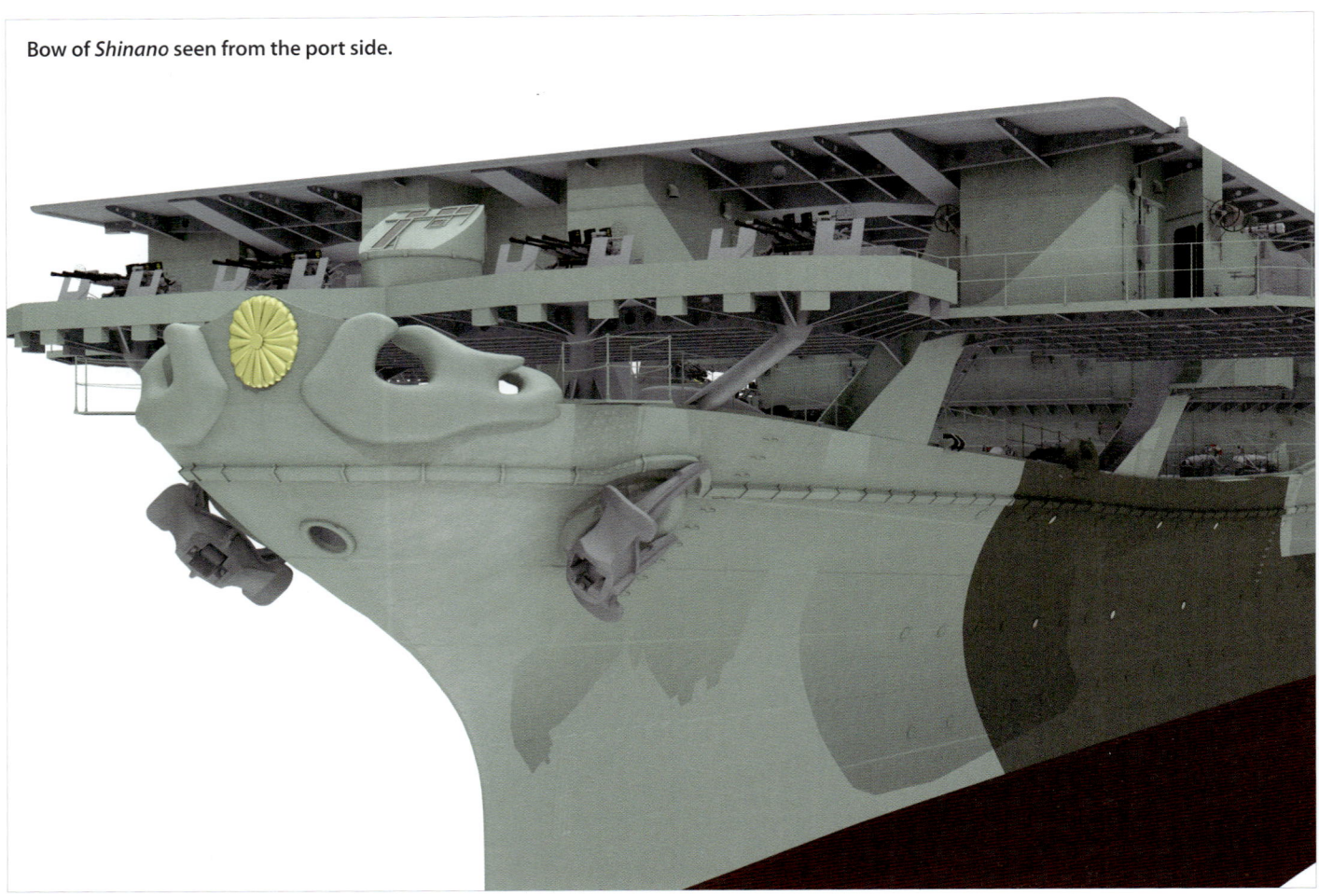

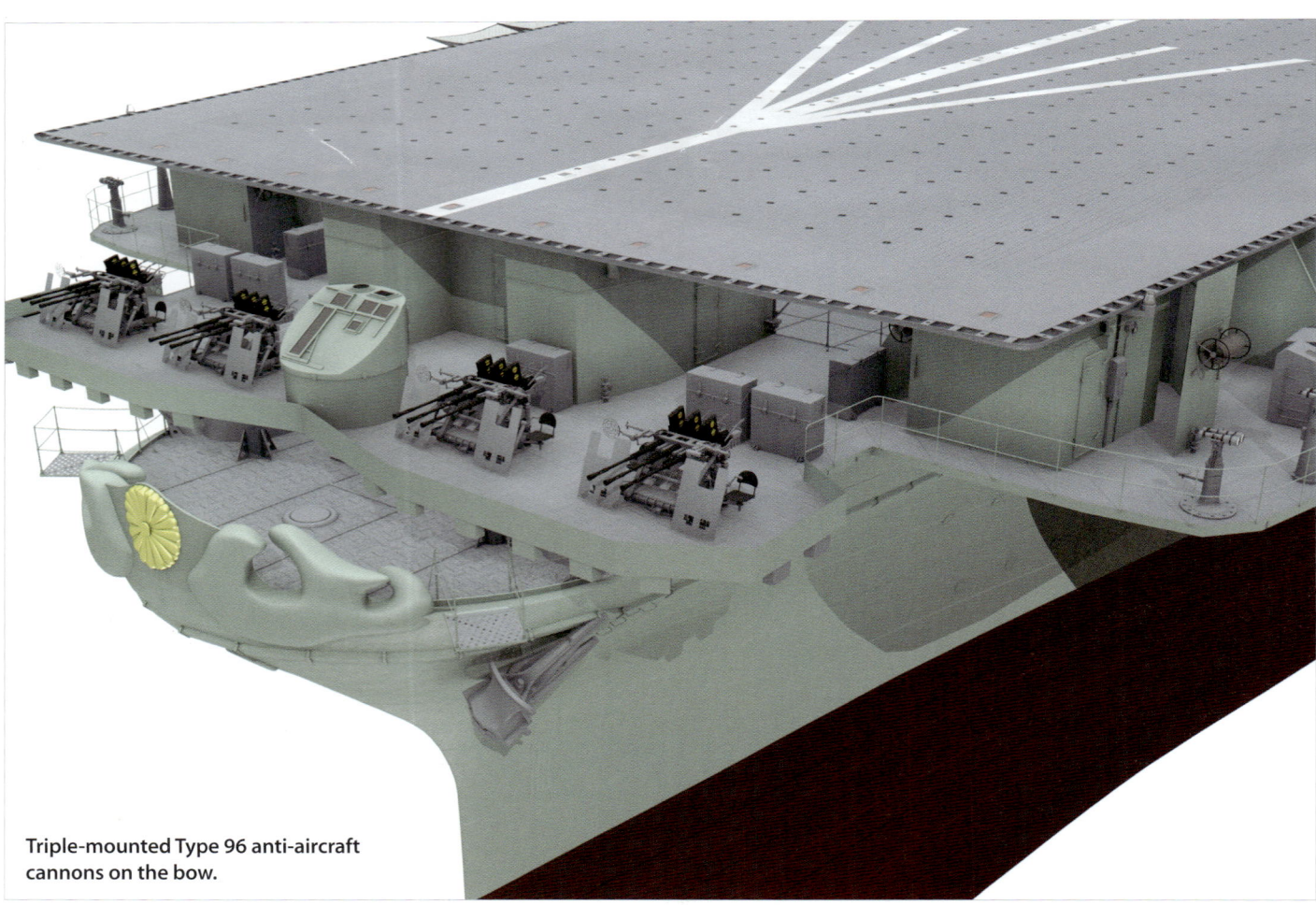

Triple-mounted Type 96 anti-aircraft cannons on the bow.

Details of equipment of the gun mounts on the bow.

Anti-aircraft gun mounts on the bow.

The Japanese Aircraft Carrier Shinano

▲ Deck supports seen from the fore sponsons.

▼ Unguided rocket launchers on the bow.

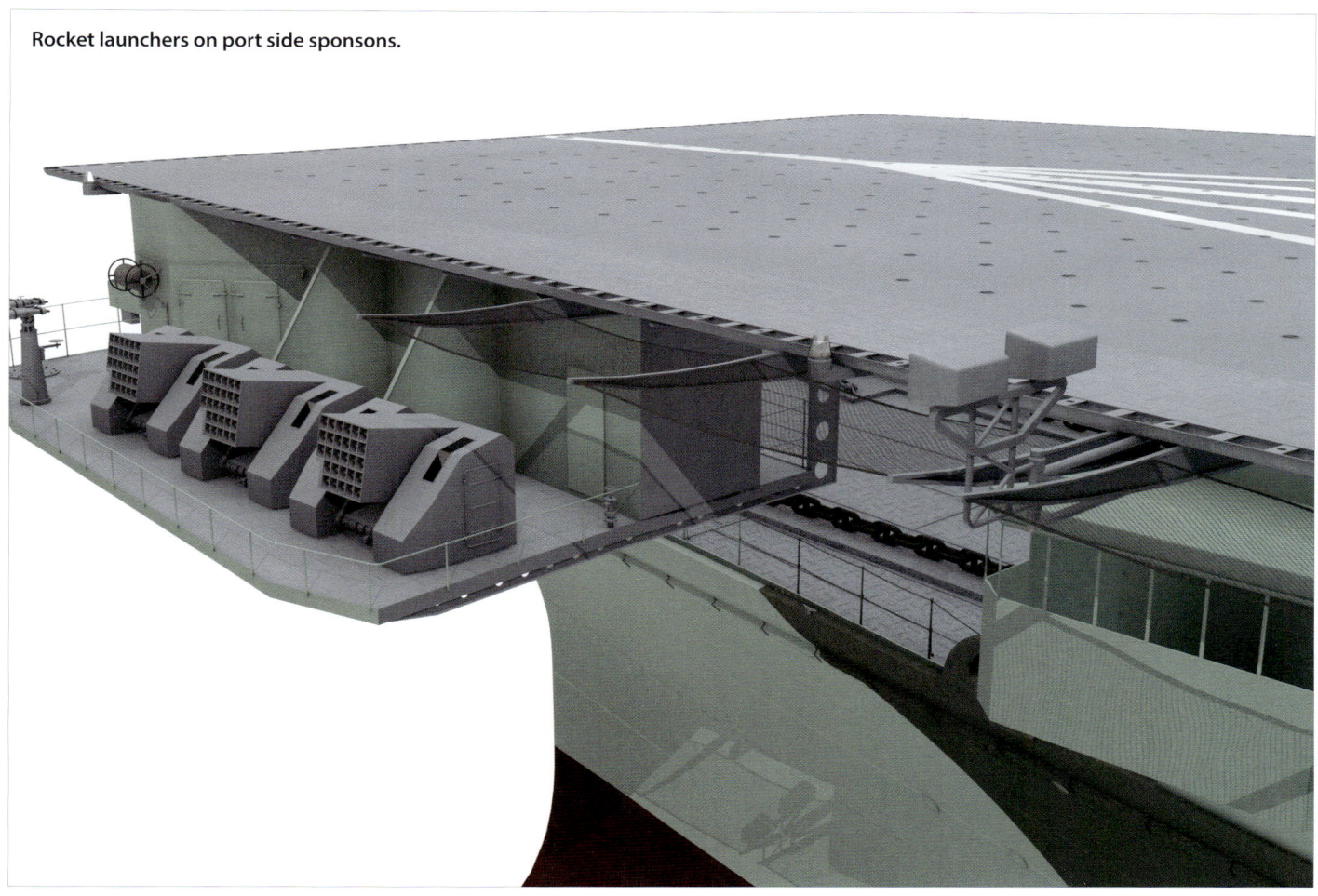

Port side seen from the rocket launcher position.

Rocket launchers on port side sponsons.

The Japanese Aircraft Carrier Shinano

Fore deck with deck beams and capstan visible in the foreground.

Port anchor capstan.

Anti-aircraft gun mounts on the sponsons with Type 95 fire control tower.

Supports on anti-aircraft gun sponsons and antenna mast.

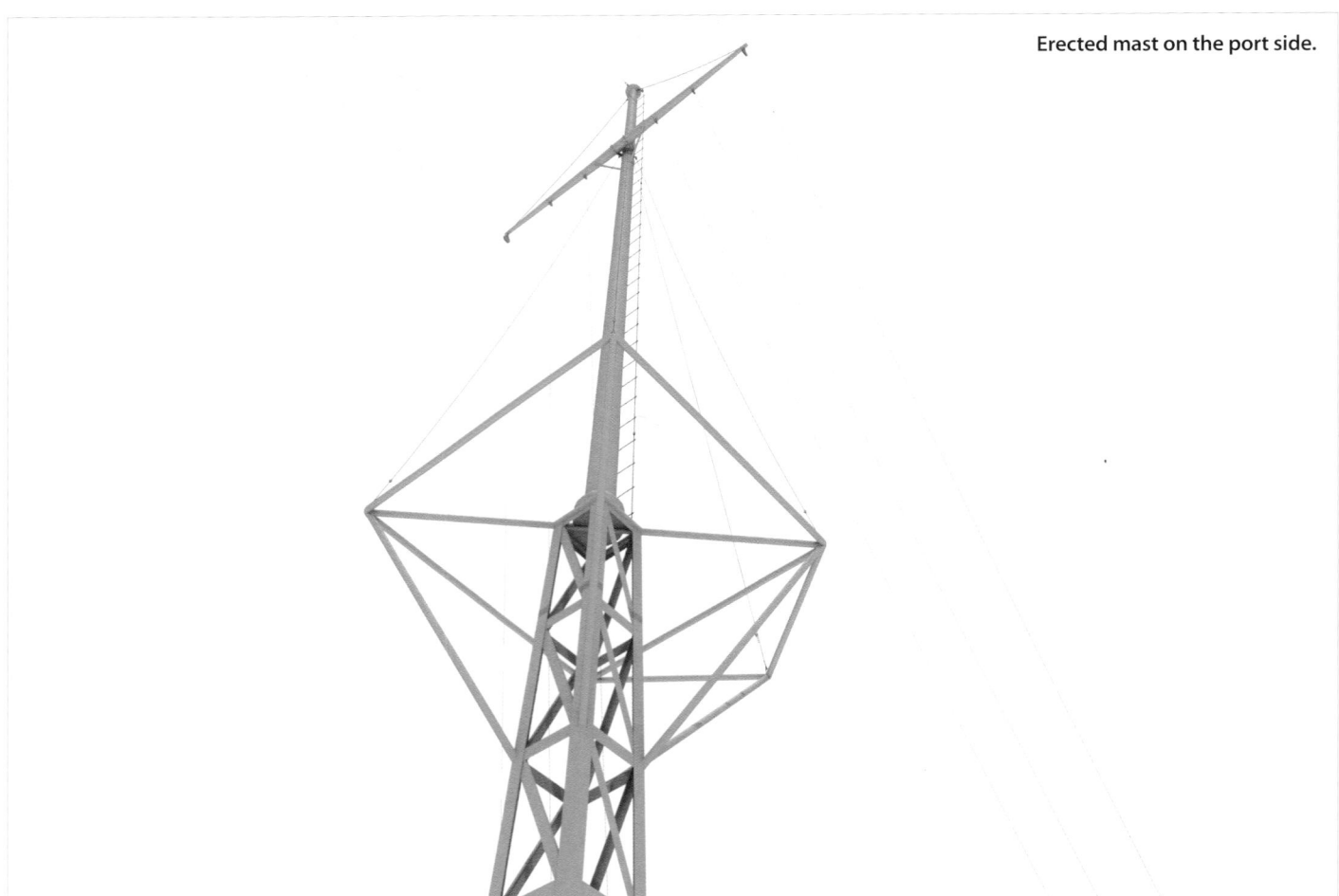

Folded mast mechanism on the port side.

Erected mast on the port side.

Port side seen from the bow.

Port side sponsons supports.

The Japanese Aircraft Carrier Shinano

Details of equipment on the fore anti-aircraft artillery sponson.

Port side sponsons seen from the flight deck looking aft.

127 mm Type 89 anti-aircraft cannons.

127 mm Type 89 anti-aircraft cannon mount.

The Japanese Aircraft Carrier Shinano

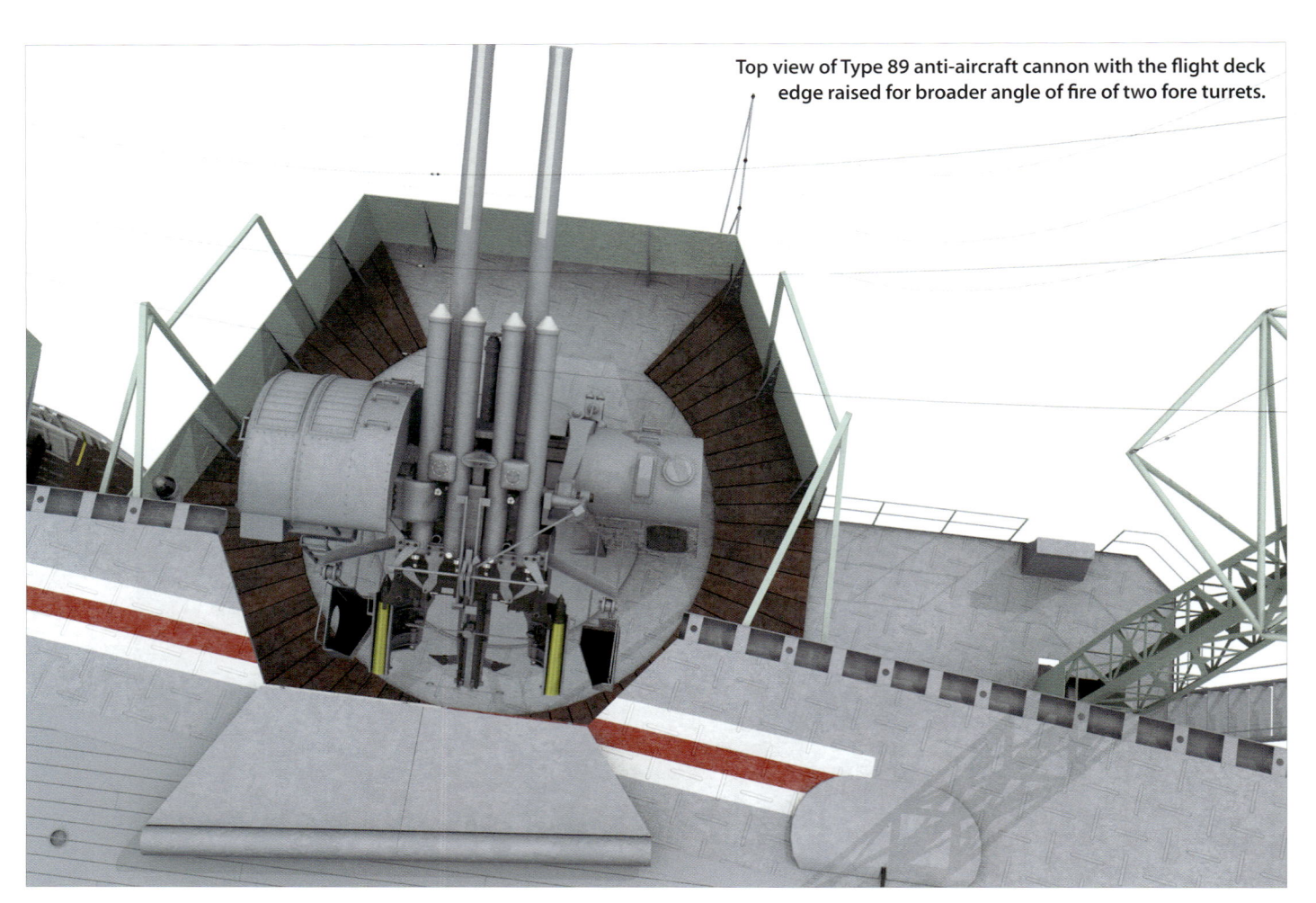

Top view of Type 89 anti-aircraft cannon with the flight deck edge raised for broader angle of fire of two fore turrets.

Right side view of Type 89 gun.

Lifeboat on the davit on the sponson below the main artillery gun.

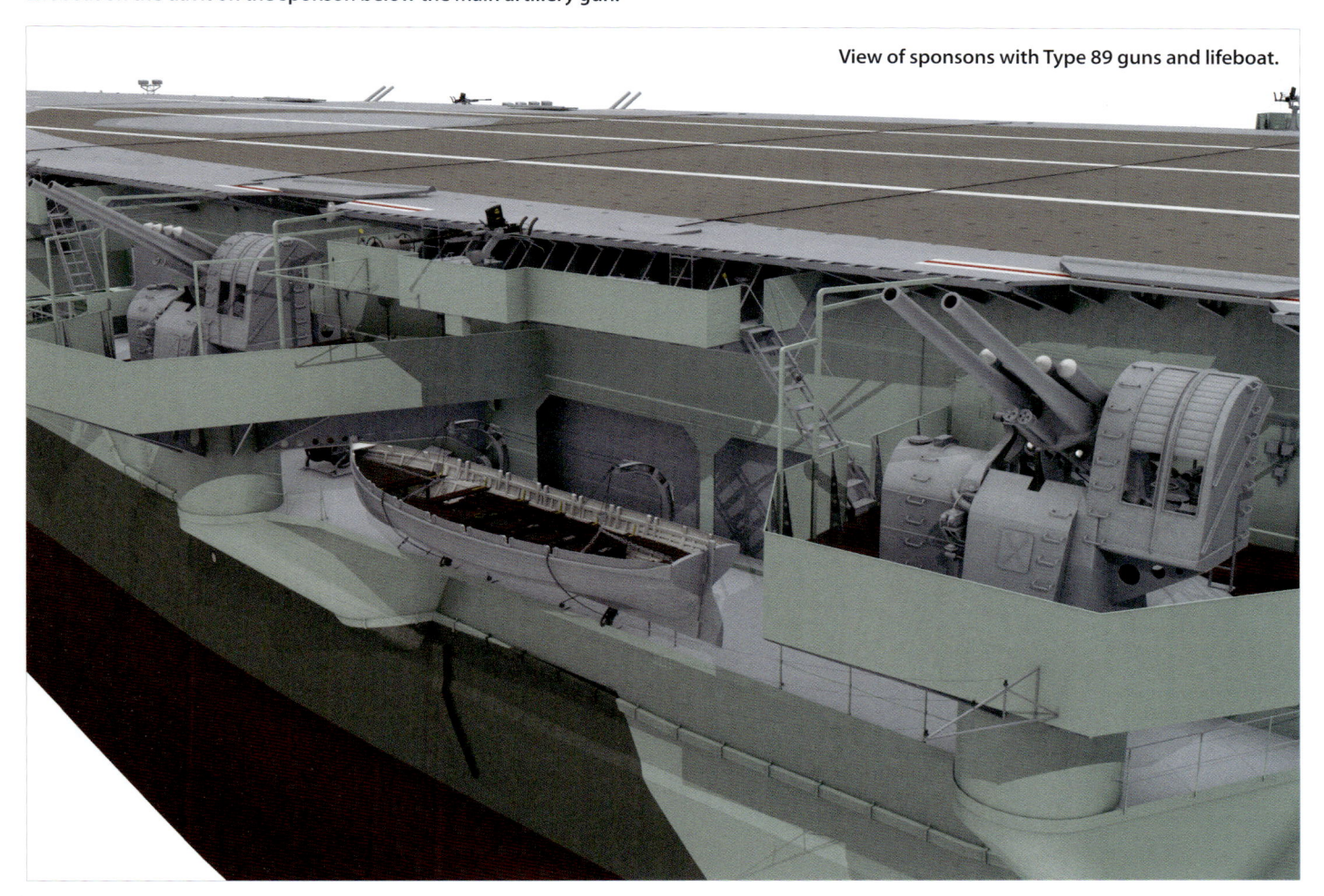

View of sponsons with Type 89 guns and lifeboat.

The Japanese Aircraft Carrier Shinano

9 m cutter.

9 m cutter on davits.

Type 89 guns seen from the flight deck with raised deck edges.

Flight deck crew position.

The Japanese Aircraft Carrier Shinano

Supports of port side anti-aircraft artillery sponsons.

Left side view of triple mounted 25 mm Type 96 anti-aircraft cannon.

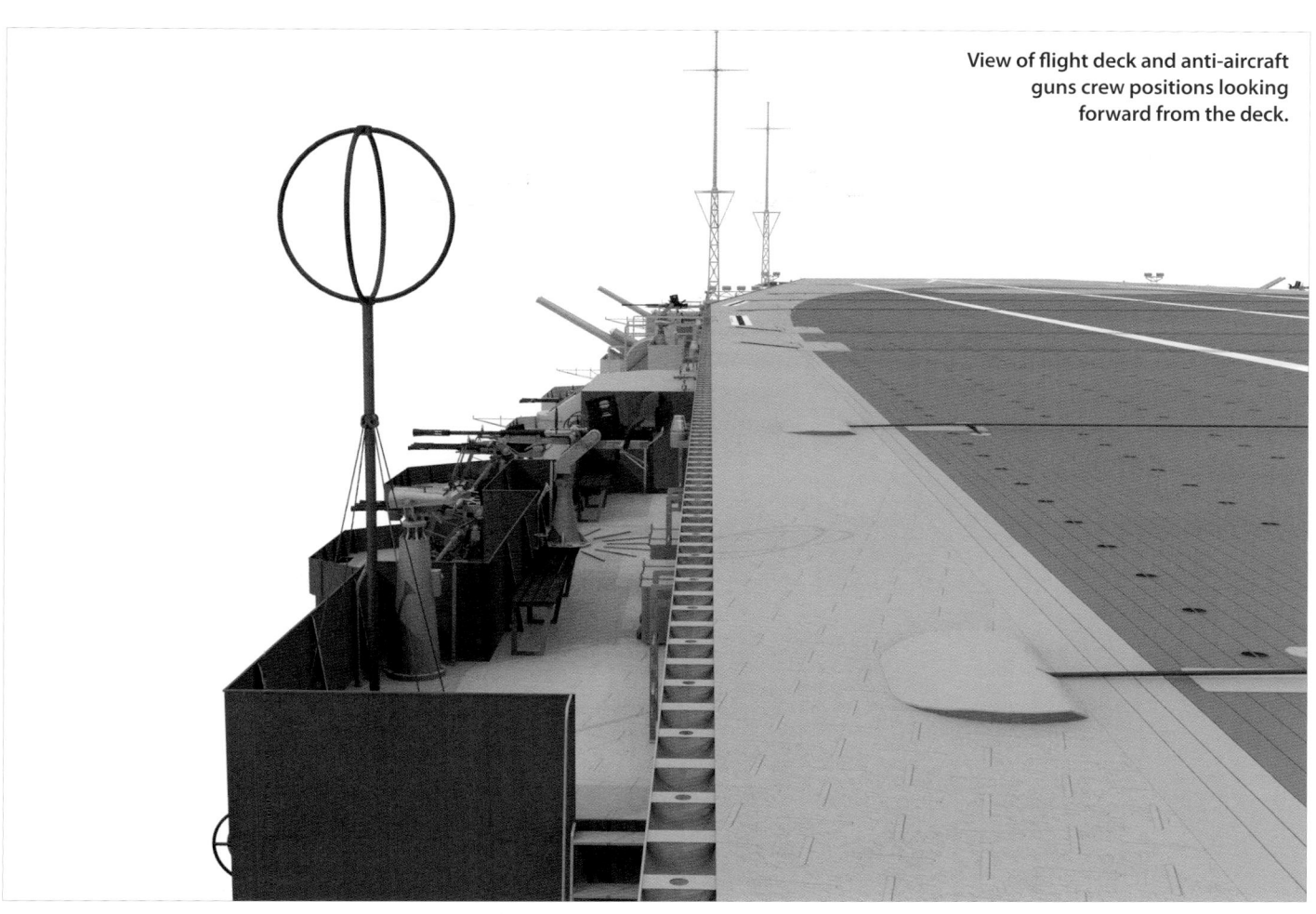

View of flight deck and anti-aircraft guns crew positions looking forward from the deck.

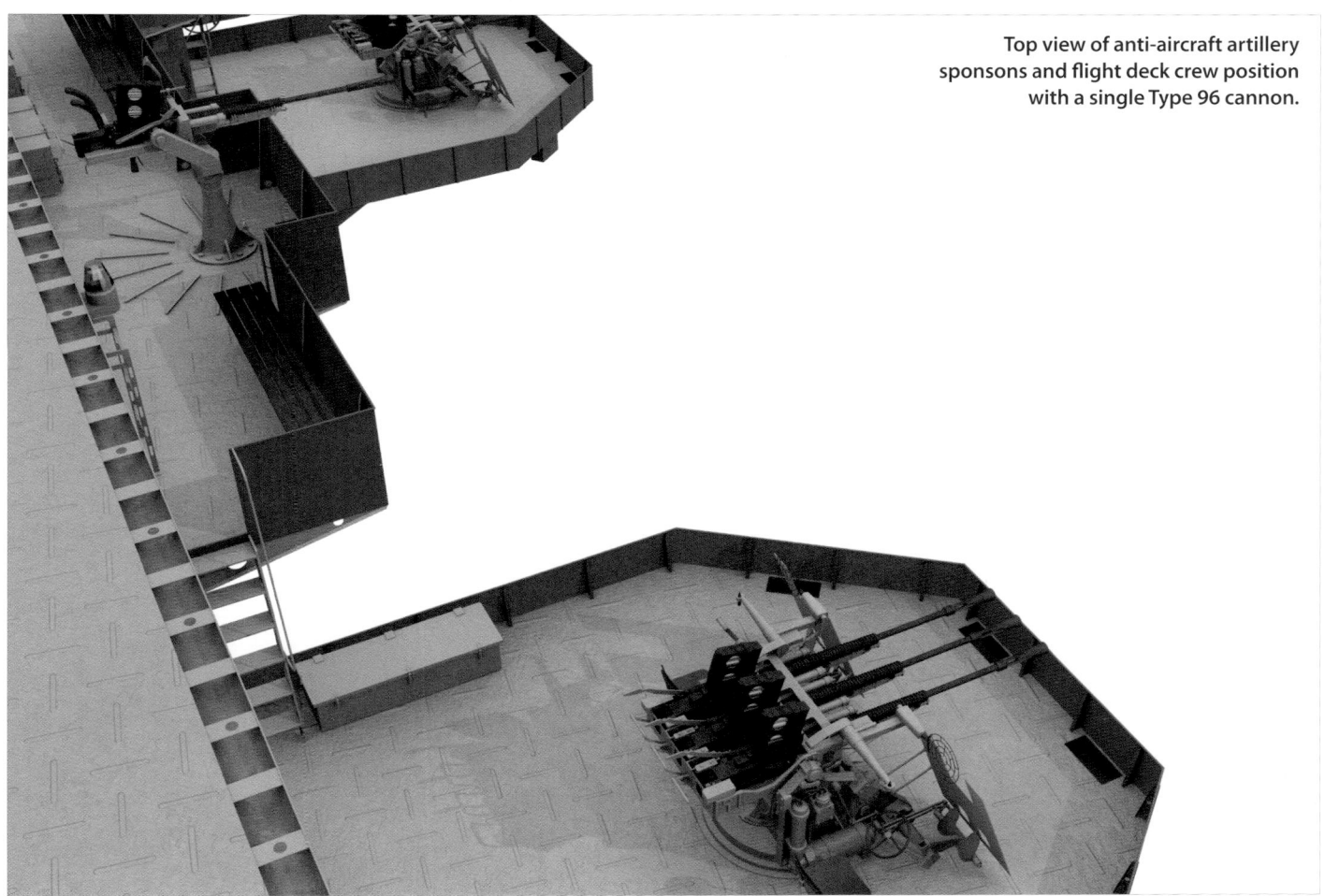

Top view of anti-aircraft artillery sponsons and flight deck crew position with a single Type 96 cannon.

The Japanese Aircraft Carrier Shinano

View of port side sponsons looking aft.

Port side sponsons seen from the water level.

View of supports of port side sponsons looking forward.

Triple-mounted Type 96 cannons on the port side.

The Japanese Aircraft Carrier Shinano

Details of 127 mm gun sponsons equipment.

3-meter Type 94 rangefinder on the port side.

Port side 127 mm Type 89 gun positions.

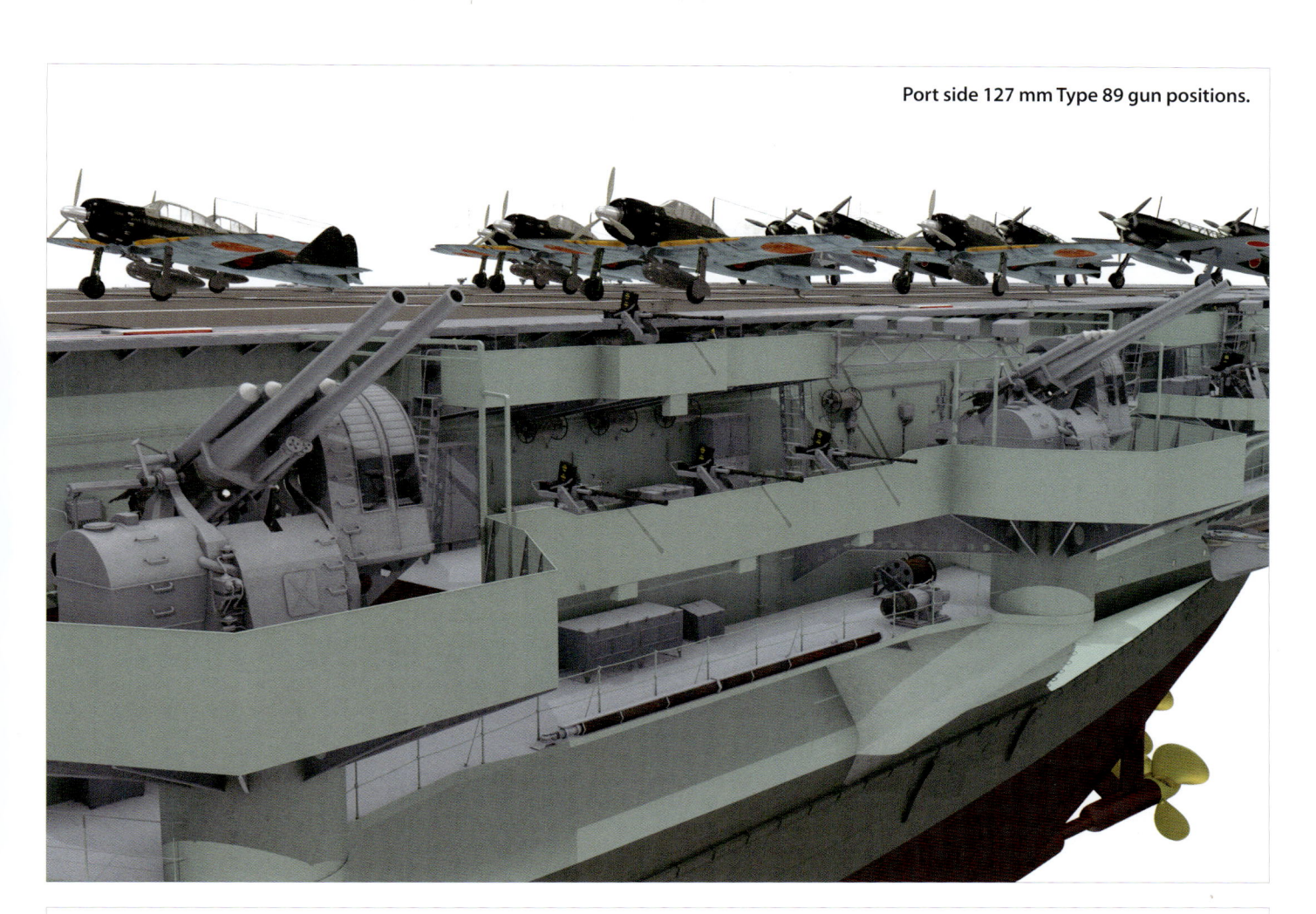

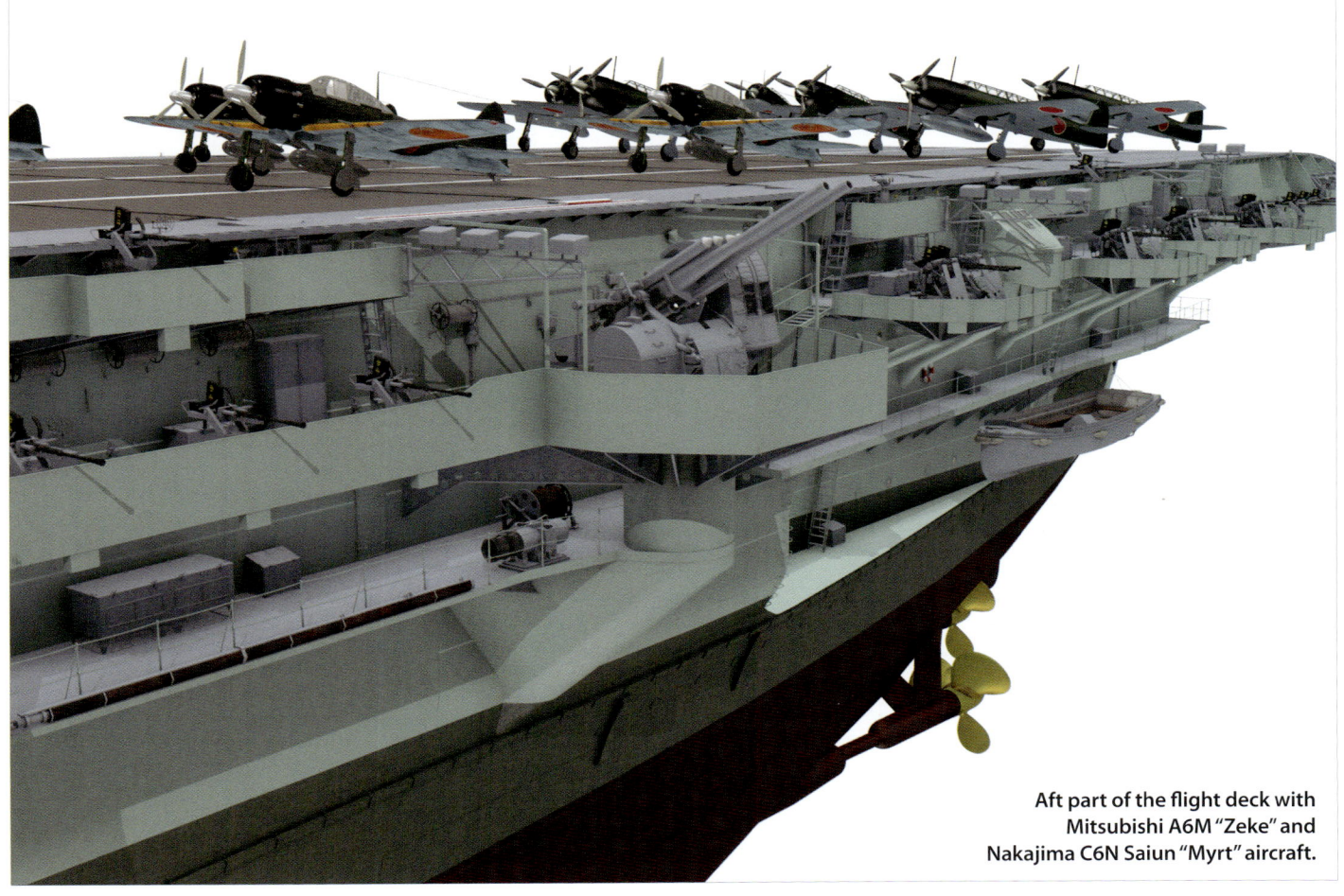

Aft part of the flight deck with Mitsubishi A6M "Zeke" and Nakajima C6N Saiun "Myrt" aircraft.

Aft 127 mm Type 89 gun positions.

Aft 127 mm Type 89 gun positions.

Port side of the ship.

Supports of 127 mm gun mounts.

The Japanese Aircraft Carrier Shinano 29

Supports of 127 mm gun mounts.

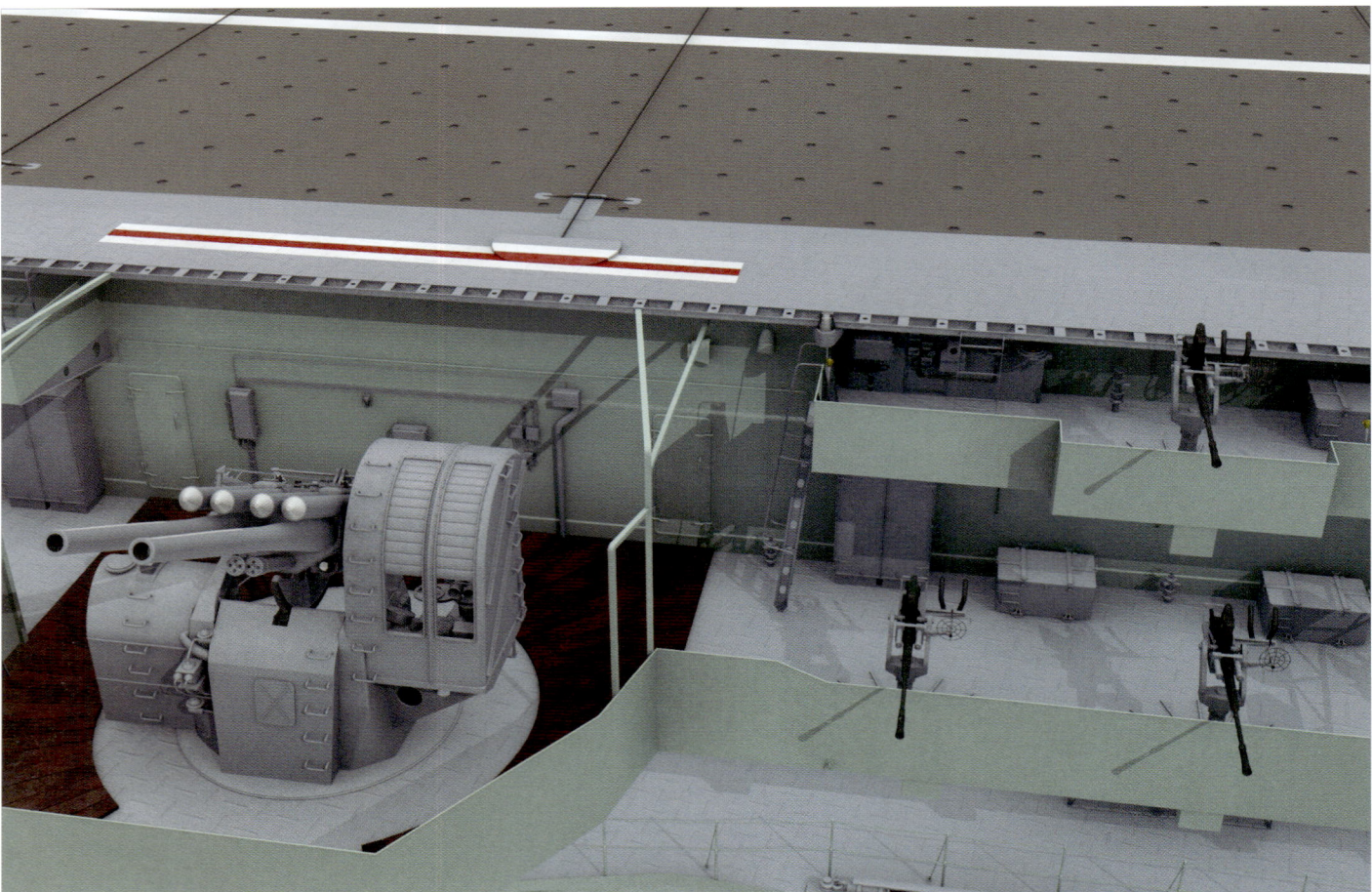

Top view of a sponson with 127 mm gun.

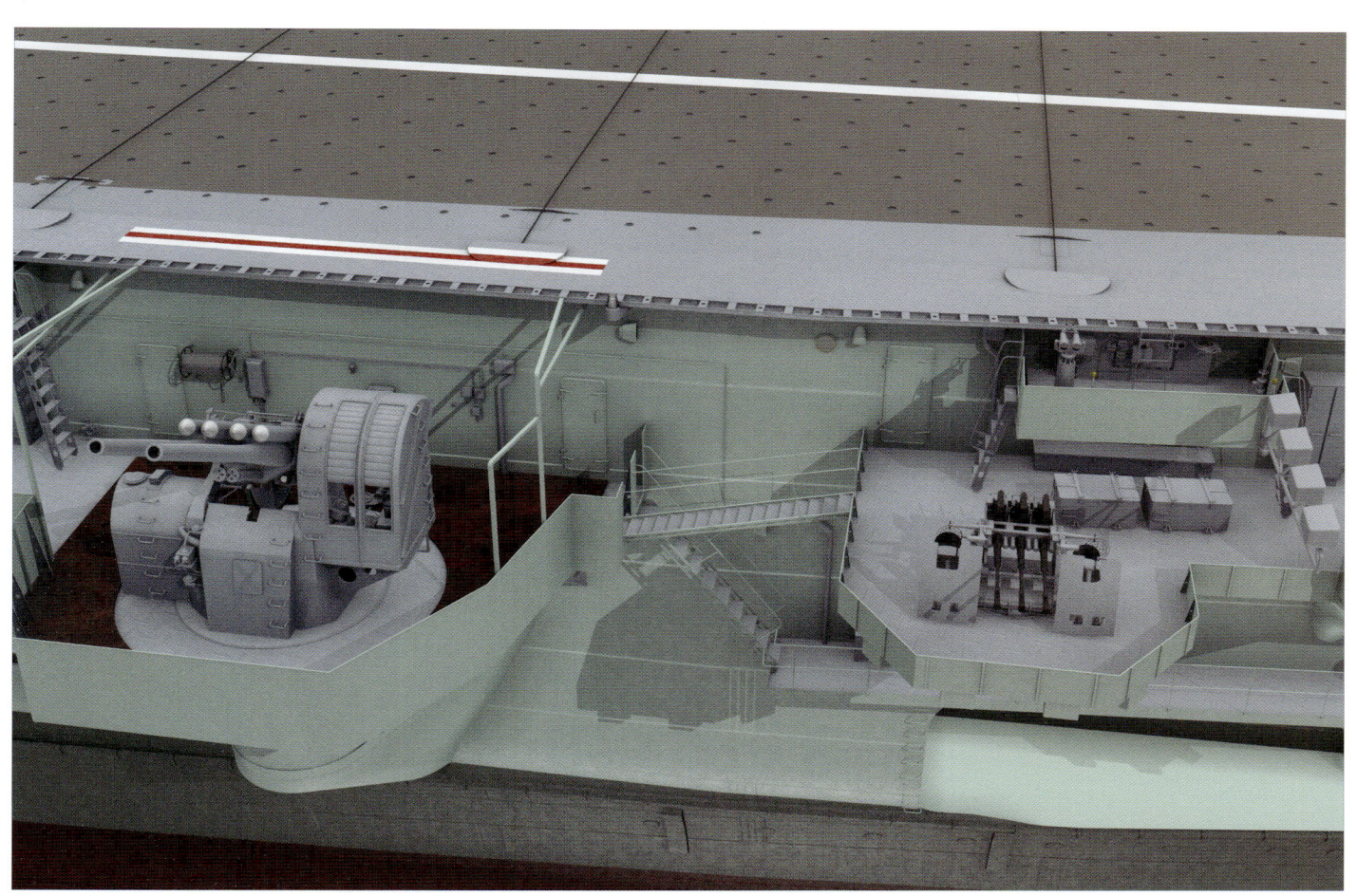

Platform junction on the stern.

Mitsubishi A6M "Zeke" and Nakajima C6N Saiun "Myrt" aircraft on the flight deck.

The Japanese Aircraft Carrier Shinano

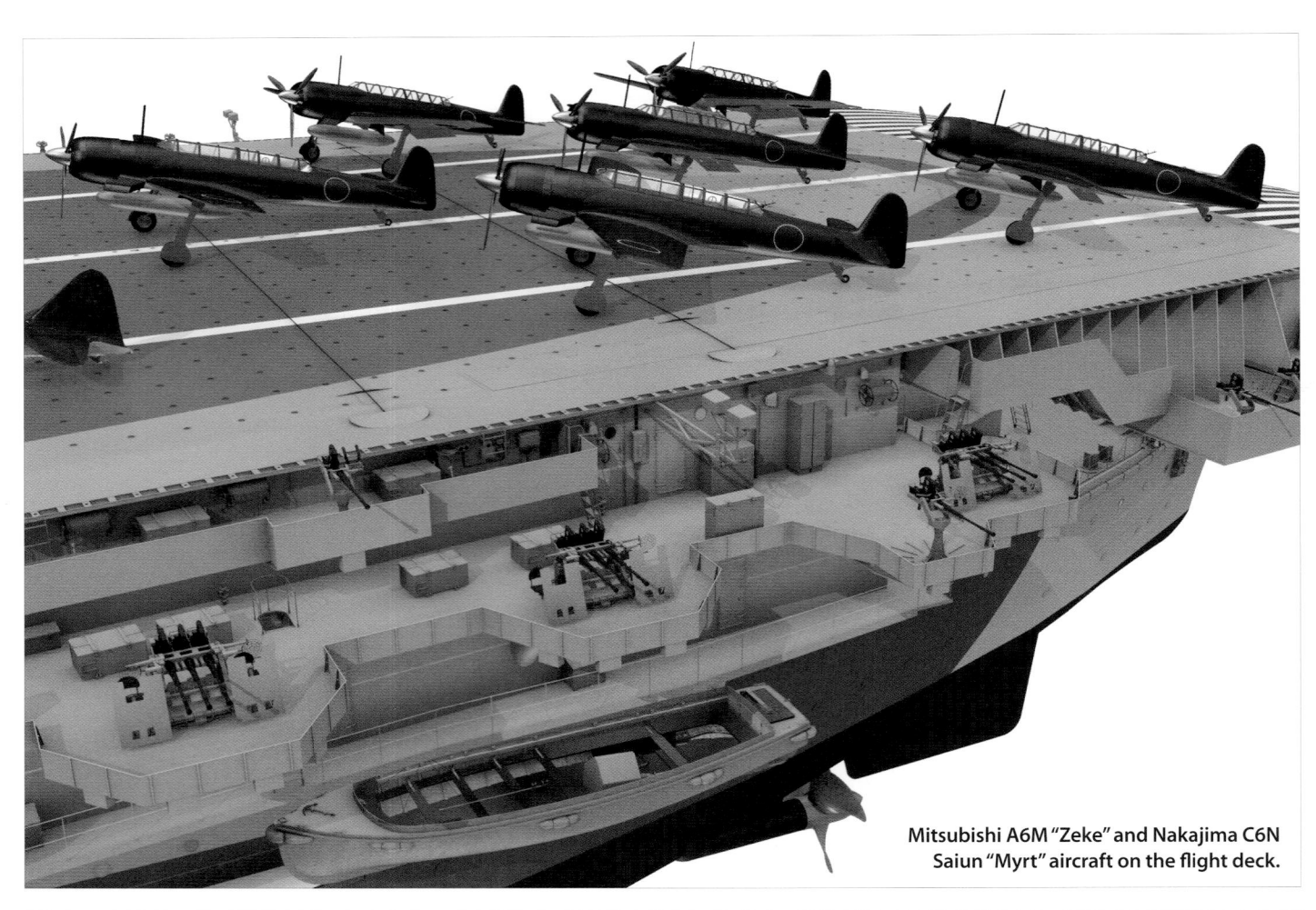

Mitsubishi A6M "Zeke" and Nakajima C6N Saiun "Myrt" aircraft on the flight deck.

Aft flight deck crew positions with 25 mm anti-aircraft cannon.

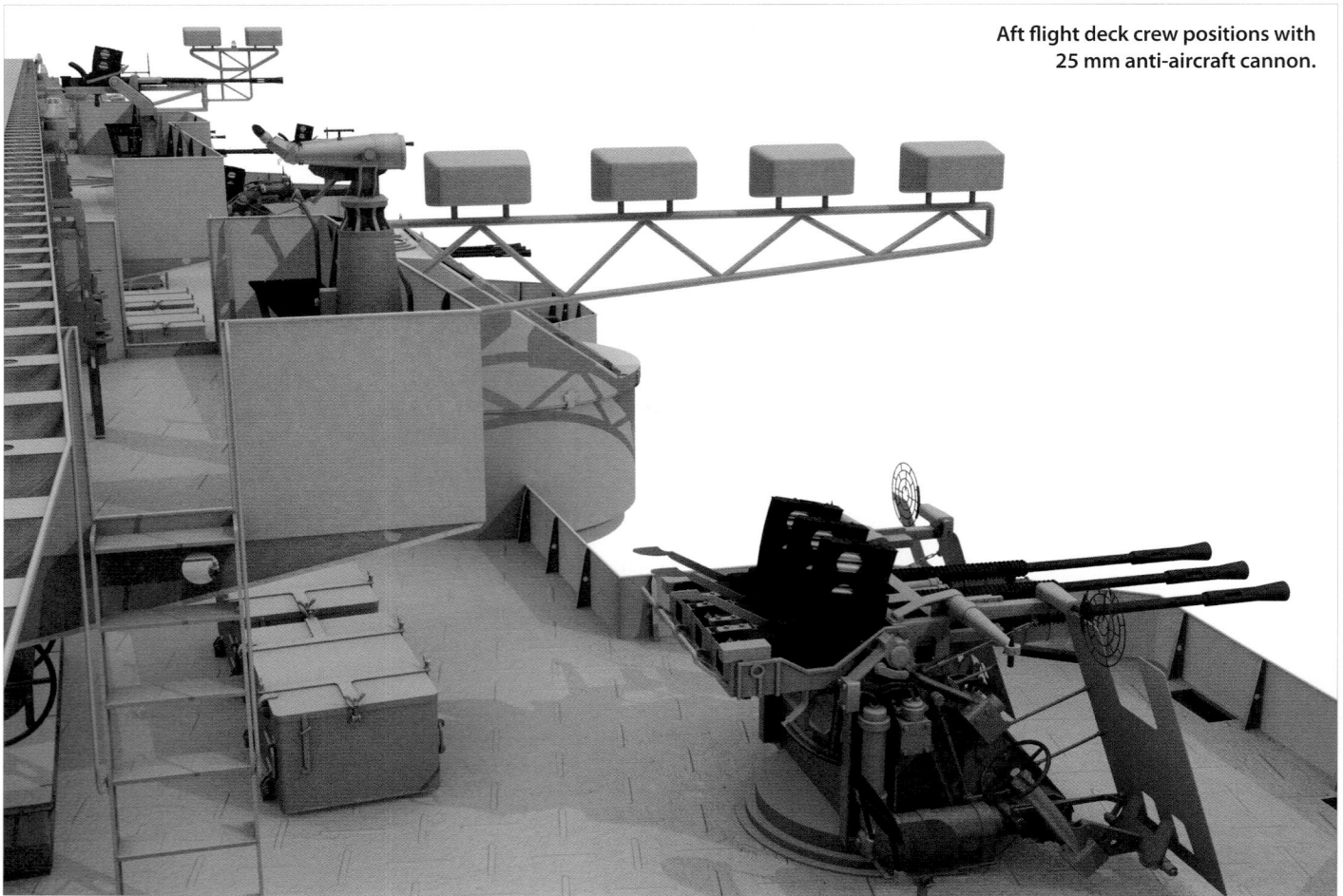

Aft anti-aircraft gun positions.

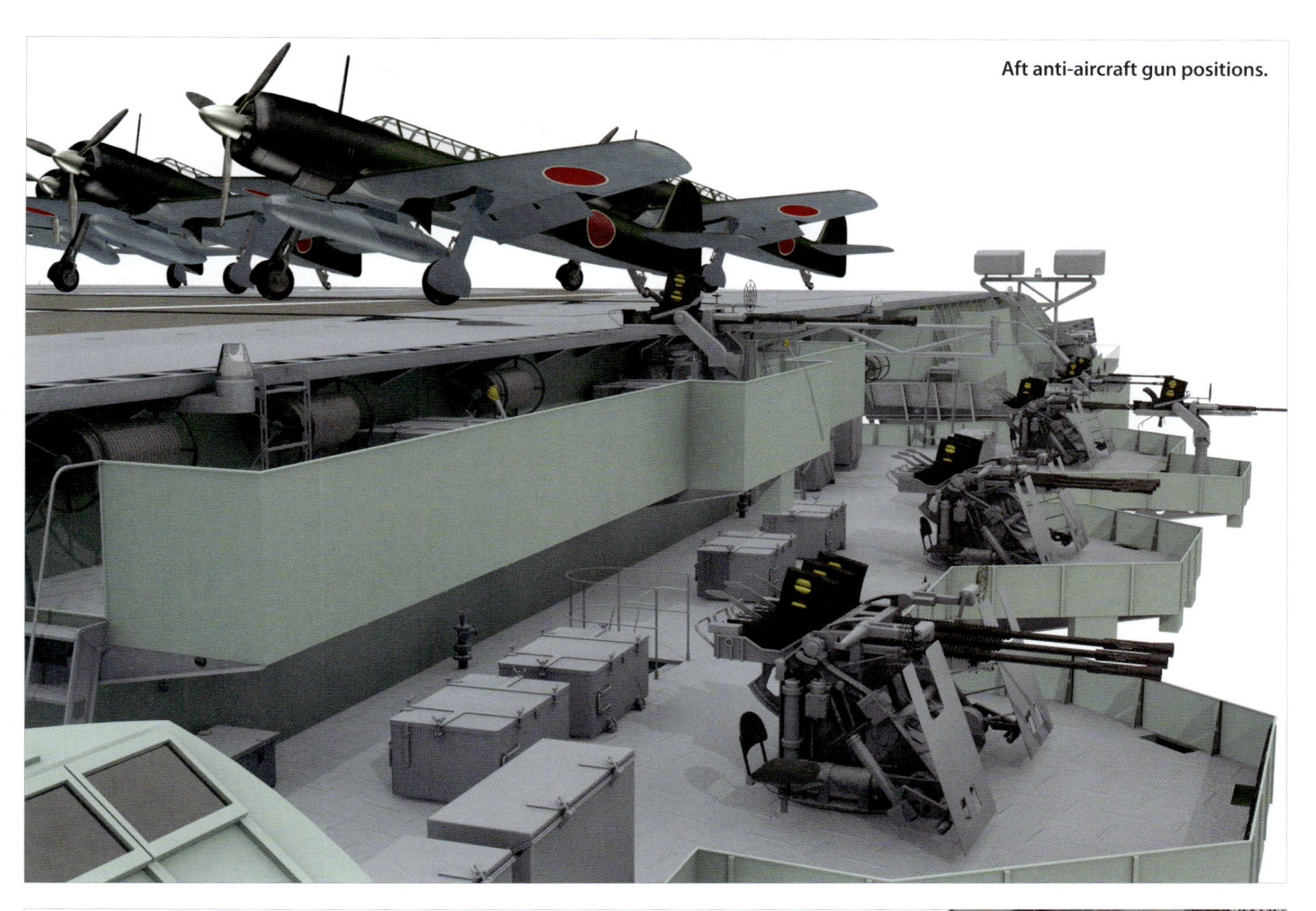

View of aft anti-aircraft gun positions looking forward.

The Japanese Aircraft Carrier Shinano

Supports of aft anti-aircraft gun sponsons.

Reinforcement of aft main artillery sponsons.

12-meter communication boat on the gantry ready for lowering.

The boat on the gantry, closed boat hangar doors are visible at its front end.

The Japanese Aircraft Carrier Shinano

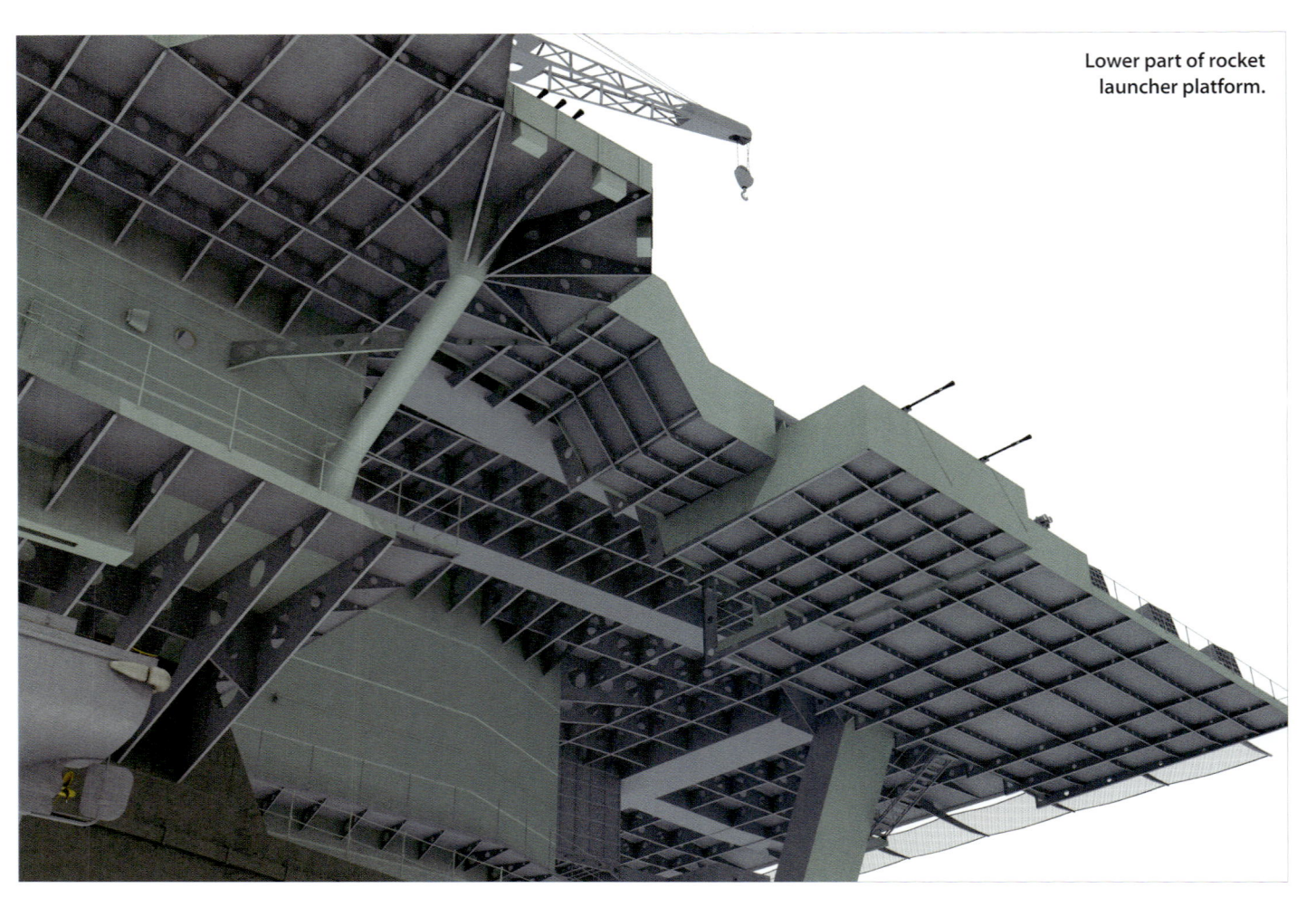

Lower part of rocket launcher platform.

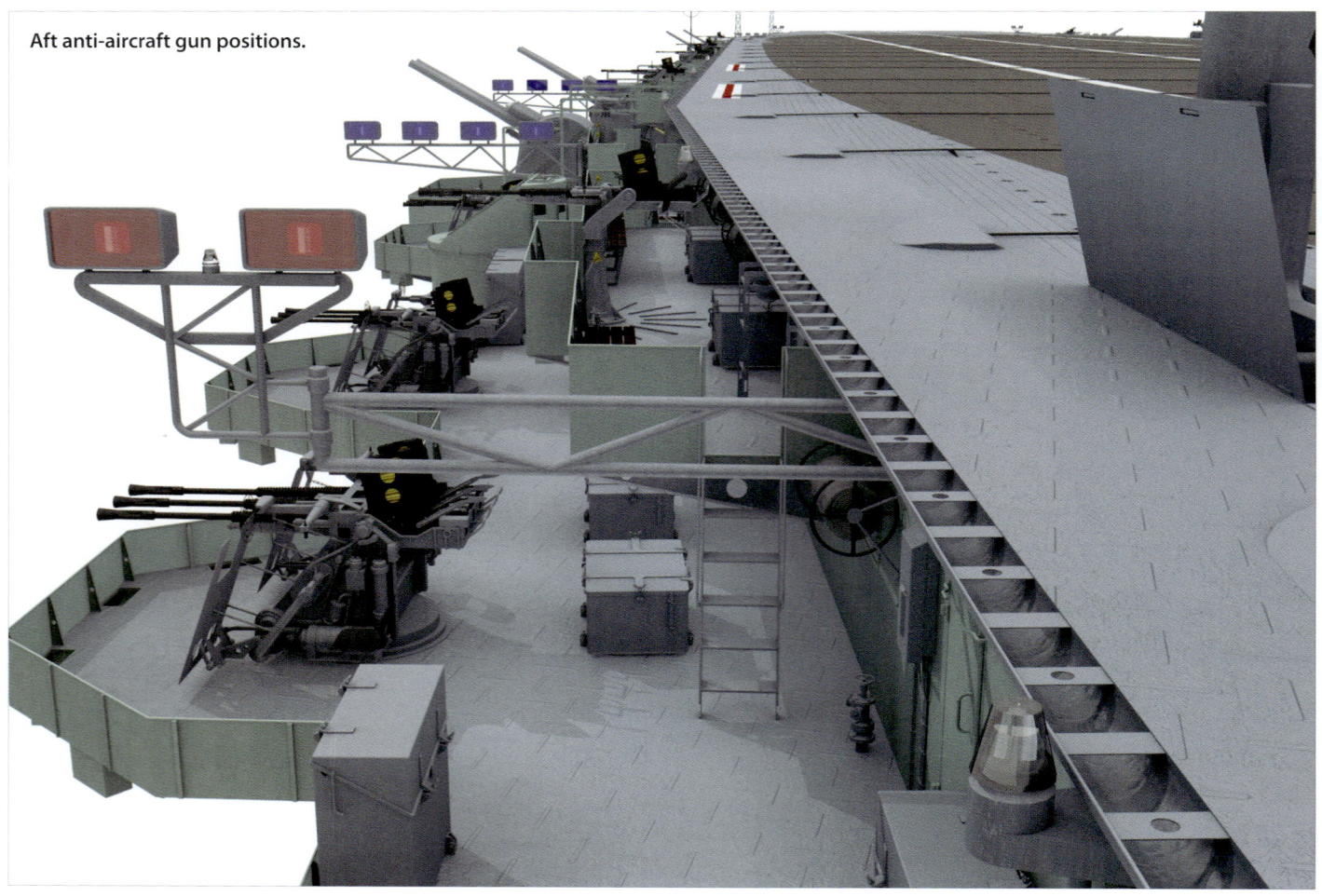

Aft anti-aircraft gun positions.

Open aircraft elevator.

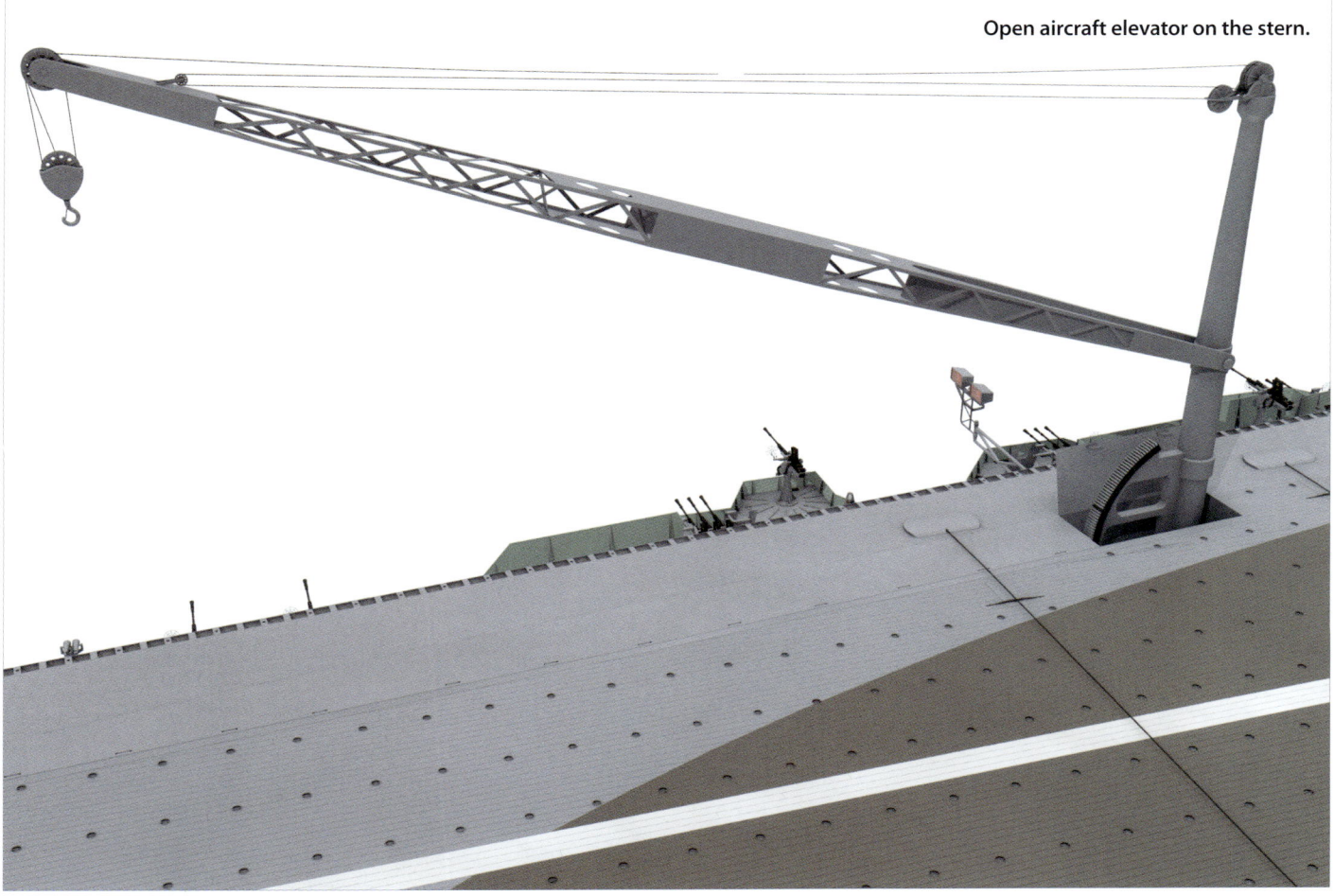

Open aircraft elevator on the stern.

The Japanese Aircraft Carrier Shinano

Aft rocket launcher mount.

Aft rocket launcher mount.

Aft deck supports.

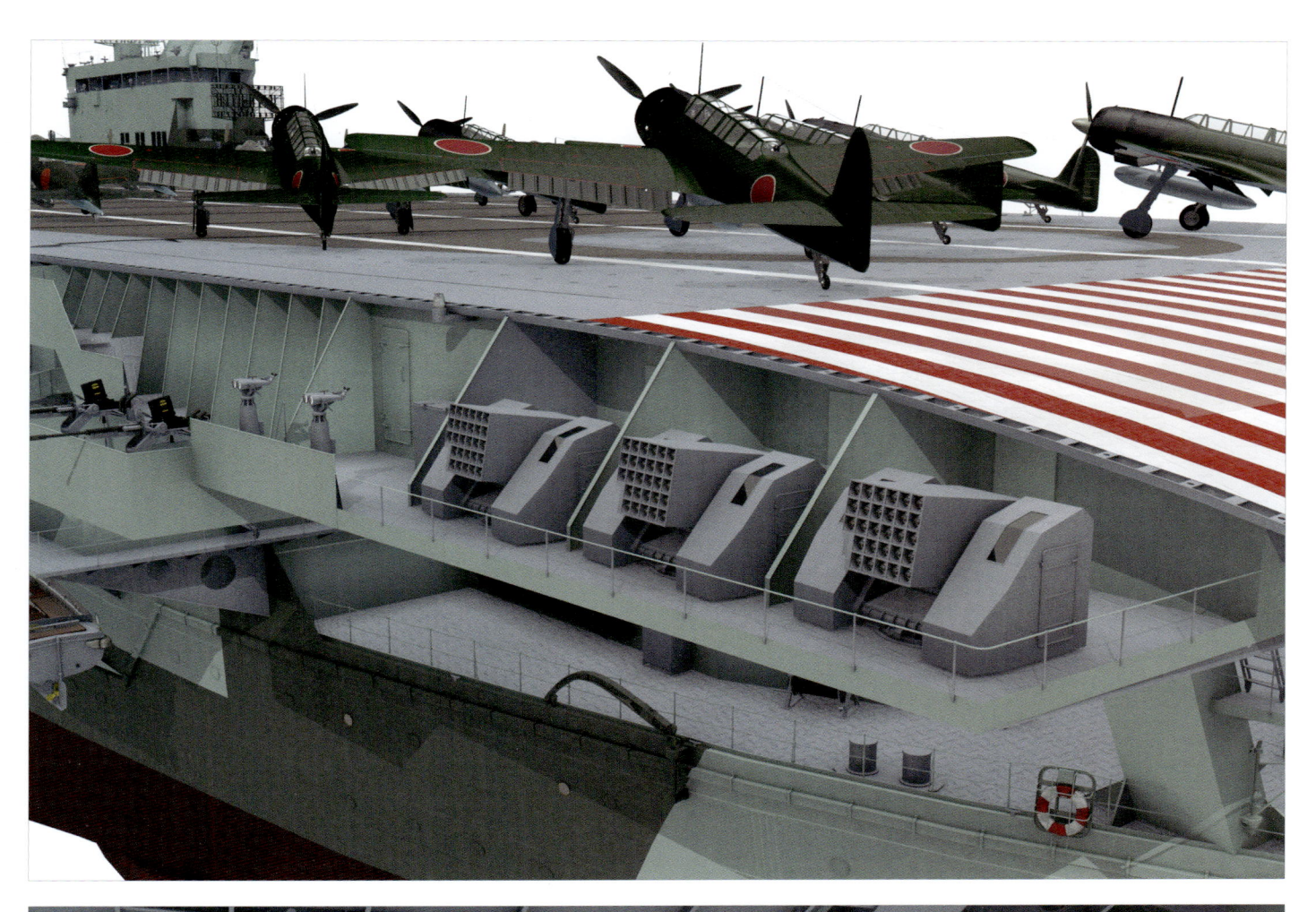

The Japanese Aircraft Carrier Shinano

Aft deck supports.

After deck with entries to crew quarters.

The ship's stern.

Aft anti-aircraft gun positions.

The Japanese Aircraft Carrier Shinano

Details of the after deck.

Entry of the rocket launcher deck on the stern.

Starboard side rocket launchers.

Details of the after deck.

The Japanese Aircraft Carrier Shinano

The rear end of the aircraft hangar on the stern.

The stern with details of supports of the flight deck.

Nakajima C6N Saiun "Myrt" aircraft.

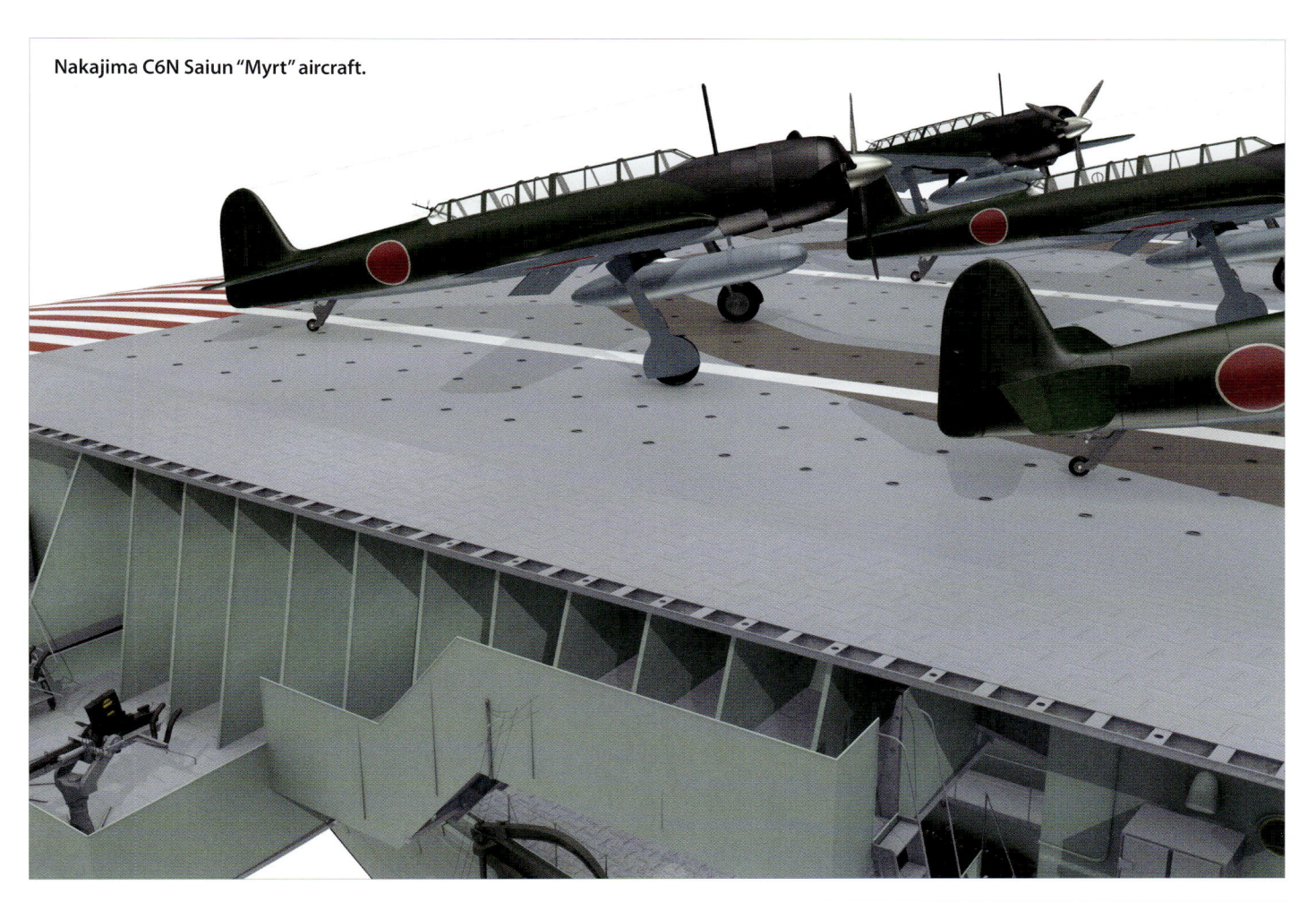

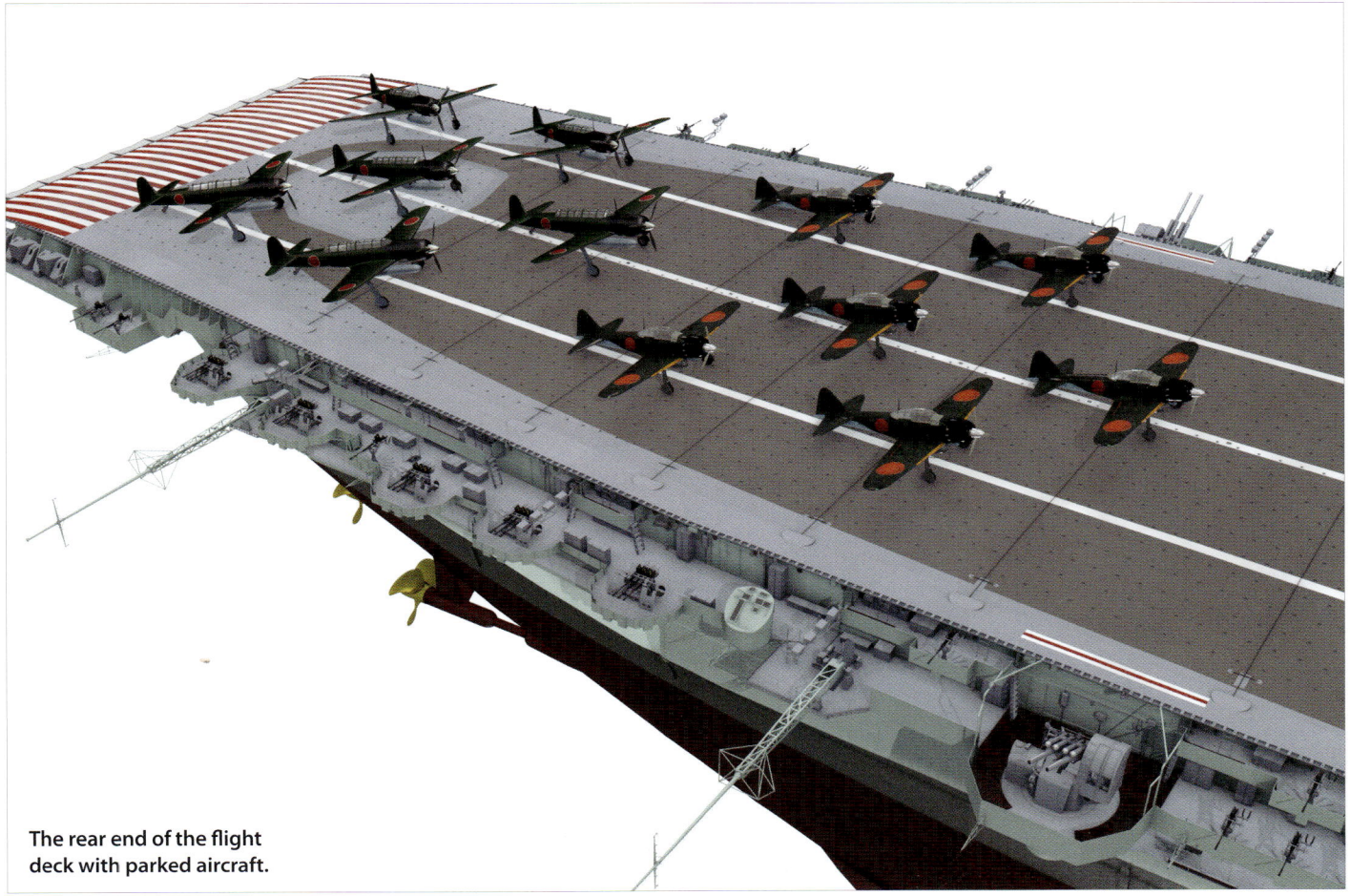

The rear end of the flight deck with parked aircraft.

The Japanese Aircraft Carrier Shinano

Aft anti-aircraft gun sponsons.

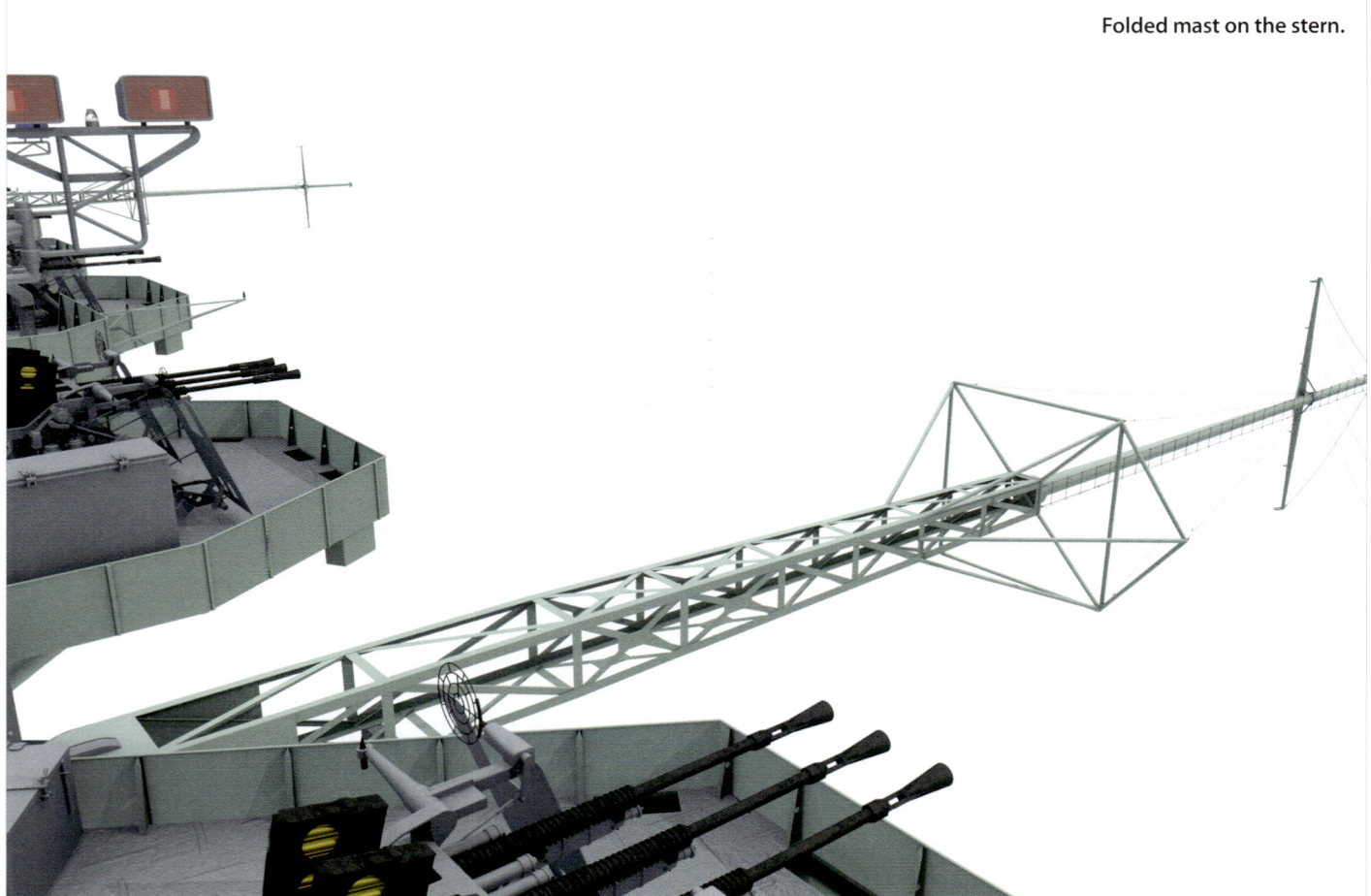

Folded mast on the stern.

View of the starboard side of the stern with folded mast.

Reinforcing beams of starboard side sponsons on the stern.

Folded mast on the starboard side of the stern.

Sponsons of the mast and anti-aircraft guns on the starboard side of the stern.

Supports of the aft sponsons.

Sponsons of the starboard side aft anti-aircraft artillery sponsons.

The Japanese Aircraft Carrier Shinano

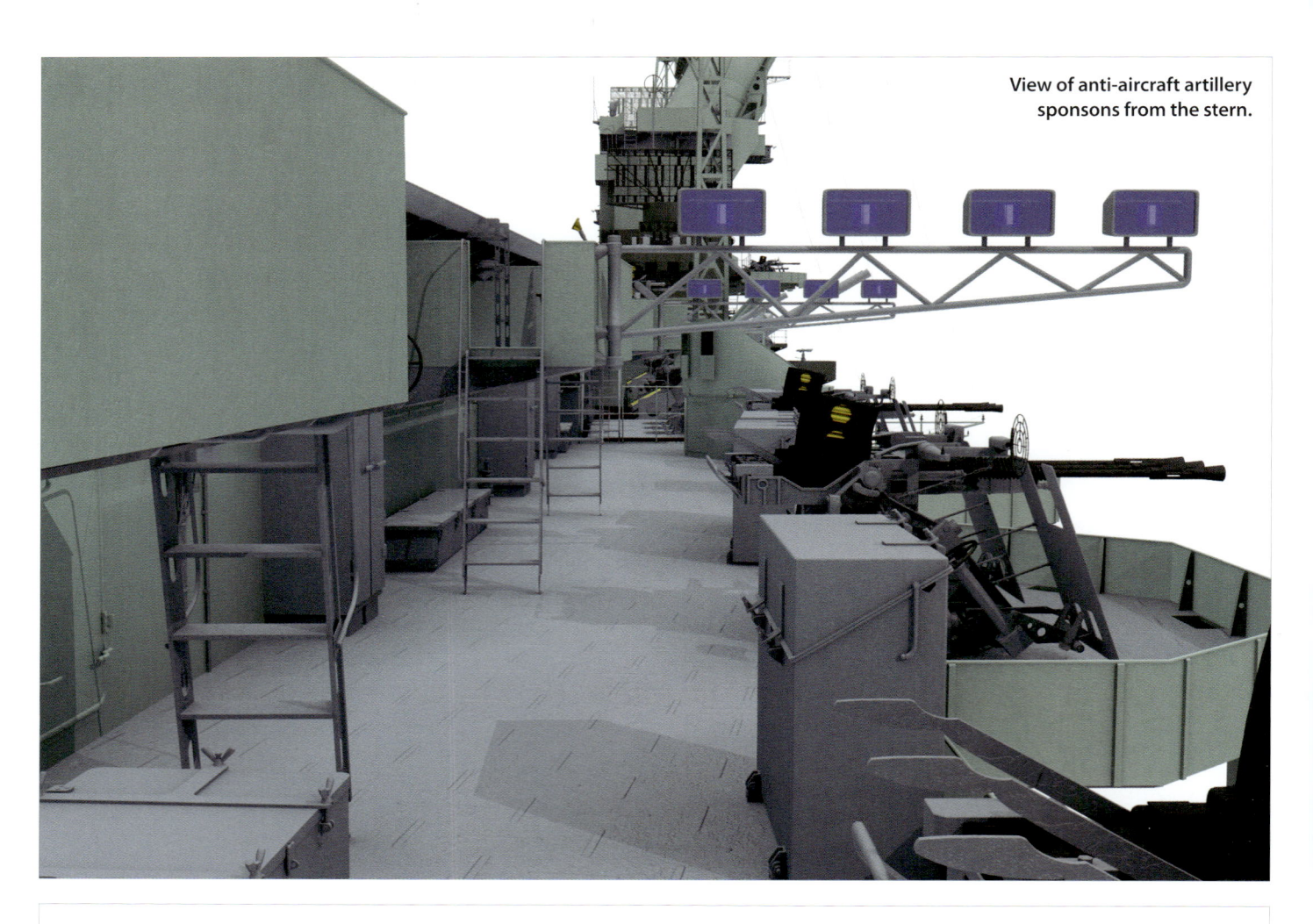

View of anti-aircraft artillery sponsons from the stern.

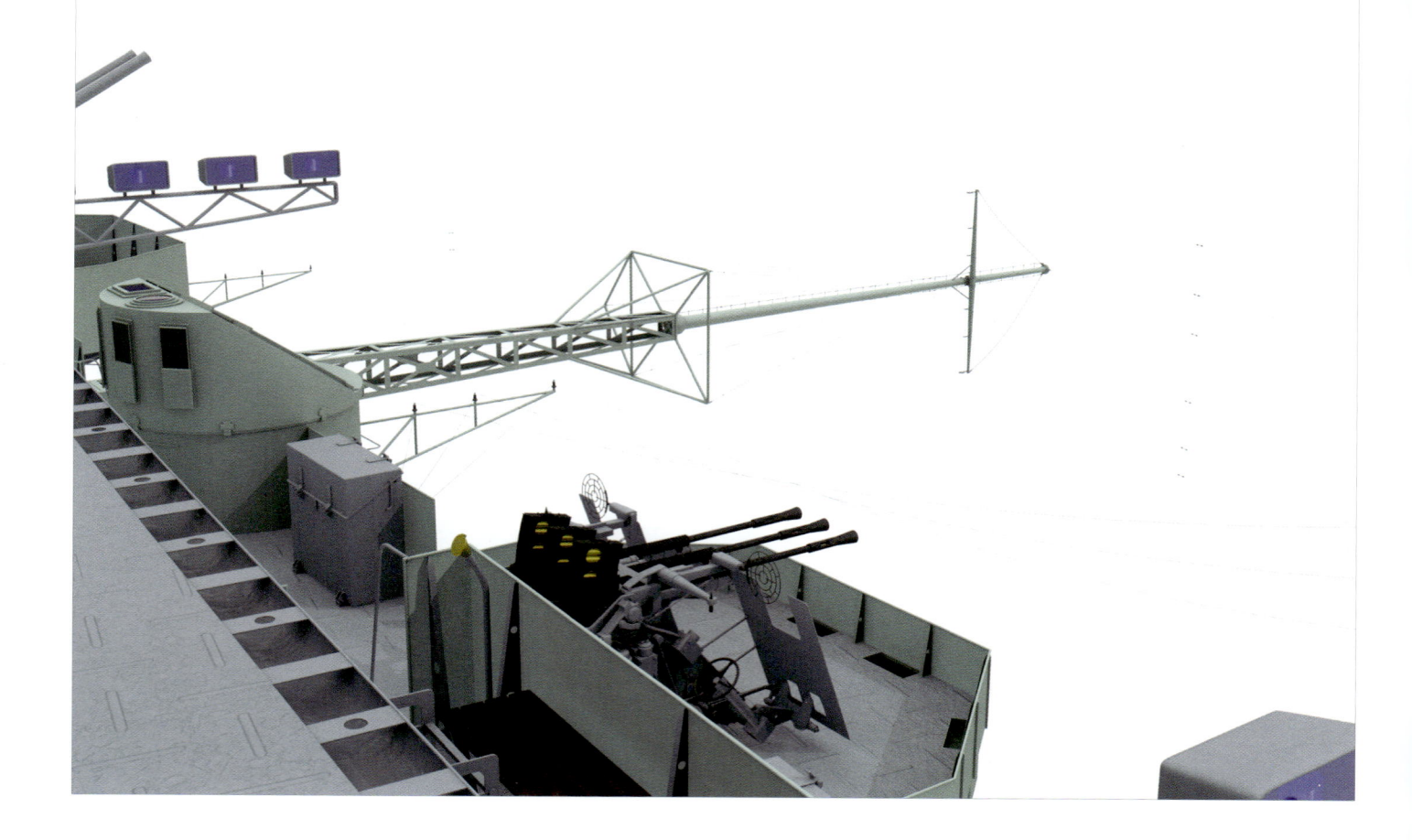

Folded antenna mast seen from the flight deck.

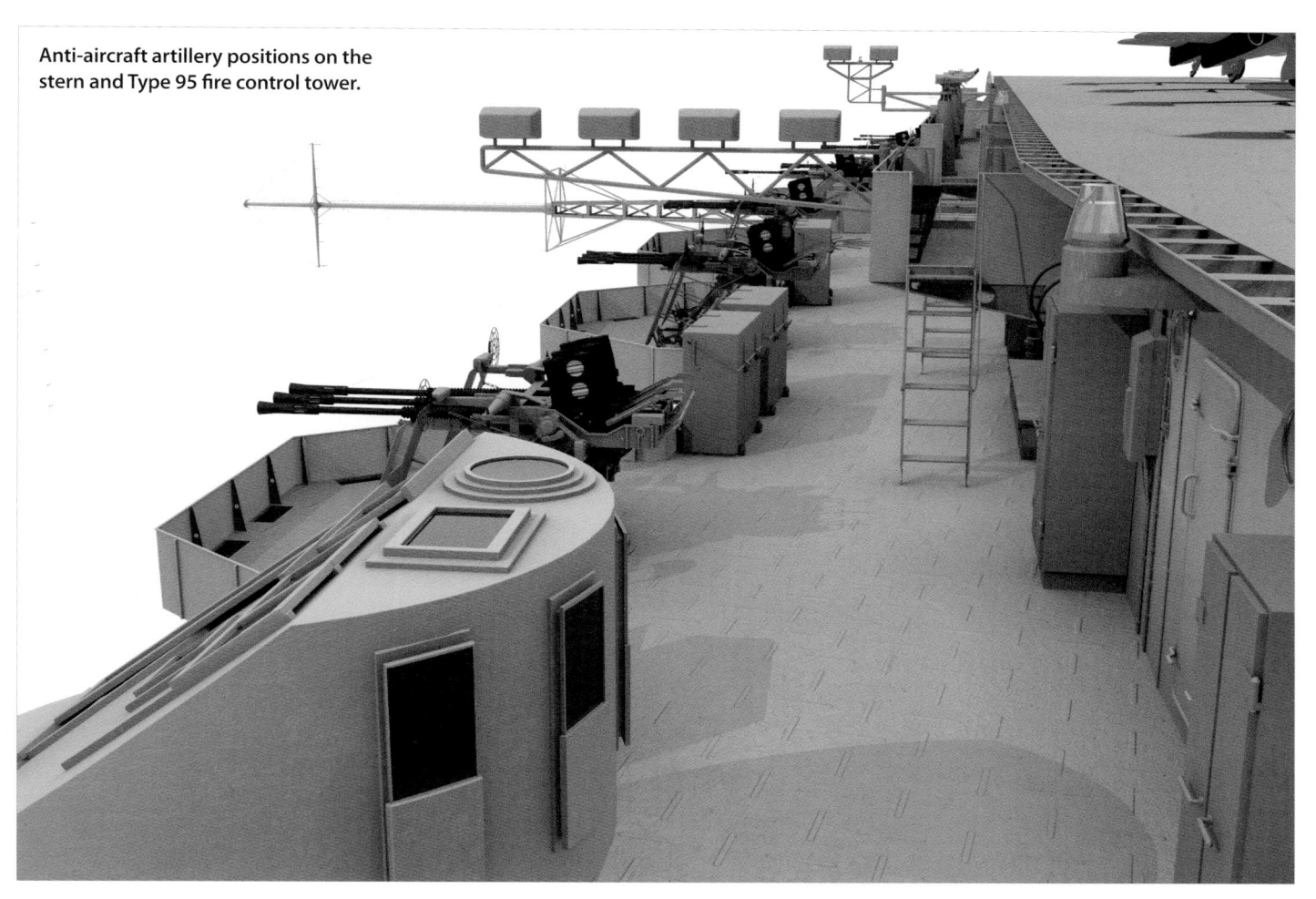

Anti-aircraft artillery positions on the stern and Type 95 fire control tower.

Supports of starboard side sponsons.

The Japanese Aircraft Carrier Shinano

Starboard side 127 mm gun positions and their supports.

View of a sponson beneath 127 mm guns.

Details of 127 mm gun platform.

A gun position with superstructure in the background.

The Japanese Aircraft Carrier Shinano

Superstructure base seen from flight deck crew position.

Main artillery sponsons seen from the hangar deck looking aft.

Sponson of 127 mm gun mount with its reinforcement.

Superstructure seen from the flight deck.

Mighty superstructure seen from the deck looking from the stern.

Front side of the superstructure.

Forward part of the superstructure seen from the deck.

Rear part of the superstructure.

The Japanese Aircraft Carrier Shinano

Superstructure seen from the stern.

Type 21 radar on the rear platform of the superstructure.

Port side of the superstructure seen from the deck.

The Japanese Aircraft Carrier Shinano

Forward part of the superstructure.

Forward part of the superstructure seen from the starboard side.

Sponsons on the starboard wall of the superstructure and 110 cm searchlight.

Supports of sponsons on the superstructure wall.

The Japanese Aircraft Carrier Shinano

View of sponson supports looking forward.

Sponsons on the rear part of the starboard side of the superstructure.

Upper platforms of the superstructure seen from the rear with 90 cm searchlight on the top.

View of the combat bridge looking forward.

The Japanese Aircraft Carrier Shinano

View of the combat bridge looking aft.

Combat bridge, Type 2 Communications Equipment receiver is visible on the wall.

Starboard side of the superstructure.

Funnel with its details.

Observation deck with Type 21 radar in the background.

Signal bridge with signal flags.

Main mast with combat ensign and Type 13 radar.

The Japanese Aircraft Carrier Shinano

Upper decks of the superstructure seen from the funnel.

Lookout posts.

Base of the signal bridge and gangways leading to combat bridge.

Lookout posts.

The Japanese Aircraft Carrier Shinano

Lookout posts seen from the funnel.

Starboard side view of the lookout posts looking from the bow.

Sponsons of anti-aircraft artillery and 110 cm searchlight on the starboard side of the superstructure.

Front of the superstructure.

The Japanese Aircraft Carrier Shinano

Supports of the superstructure.

Lookout posts in the front of the superstructure.

Triple mounted 25 mm Type 96 cannon on a sponson in front of the superstructure.

View of forward sponsons on the starboard.

The Japanese Aircraft Carrier Shinano

Superstructure seen from the bow.

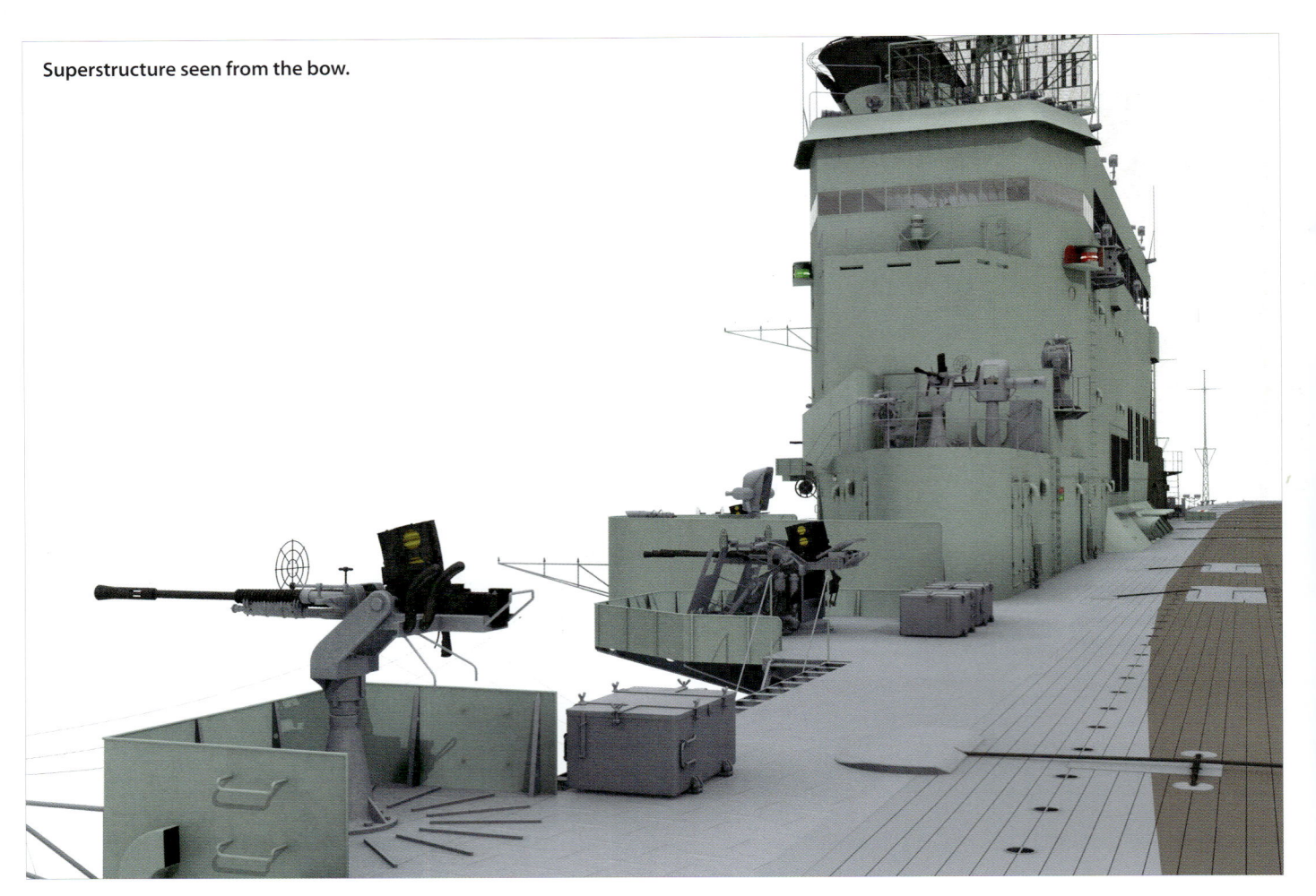

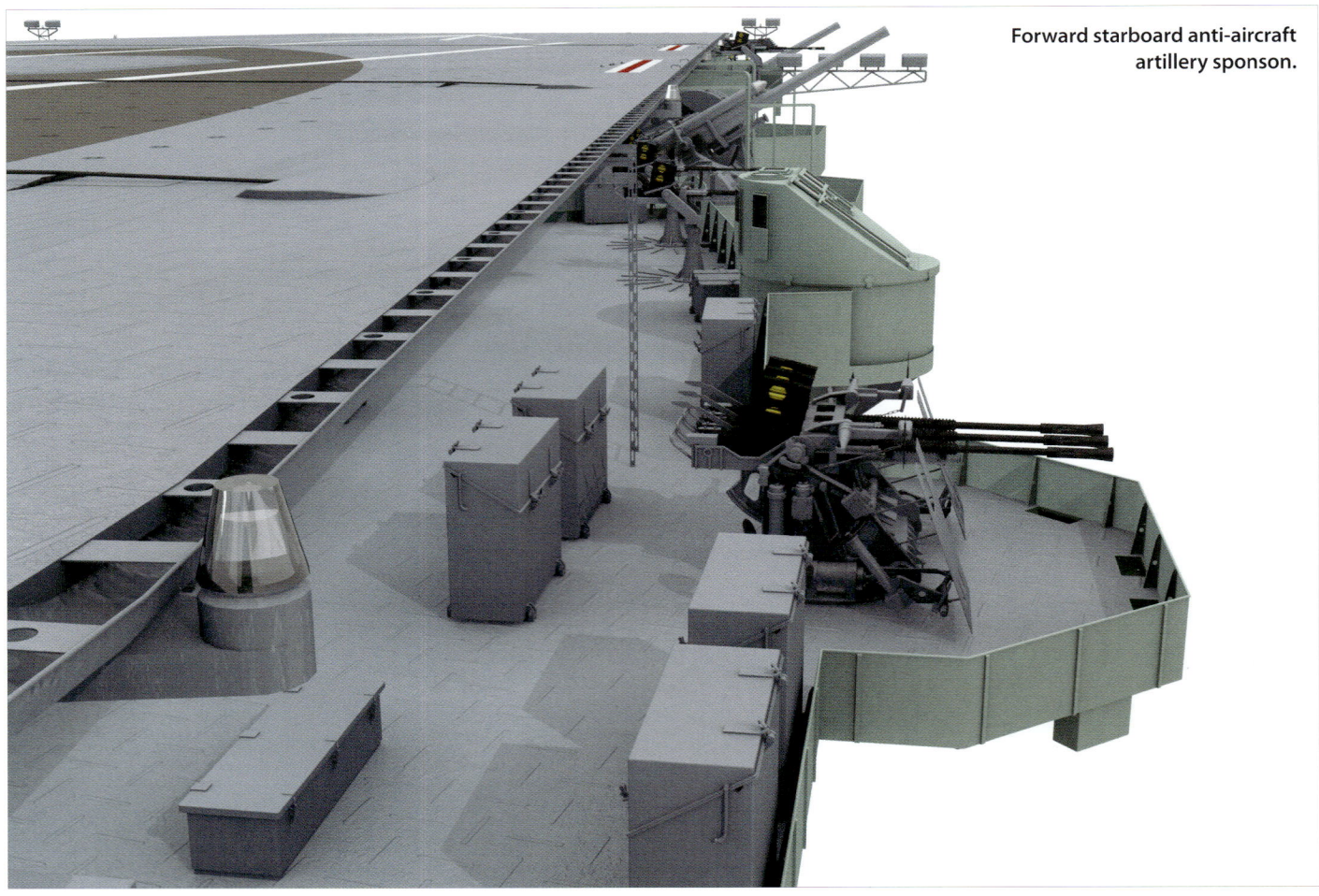

Forward starboard anti-aircraft artillery sponson.

Details of the sponson.

Single Type 96 cannons on the forward sponson seen from the bow.

The Japanese Aircraft Carrier Shinano

Forward starboard sponsons of 127 mm Type 89 guns.

9 meter cutter on the davit.

Minesweep floats on the fore deck.

Anchor chain capstans.

The Japanese Aircraft Carrier Shinano

127 mm Type 89 guns on forward starboard sponsons.

Front wall of the hangar with capstans on the fore deck.

Bow section of the hull.

Rocket launchers on the bow sponson.

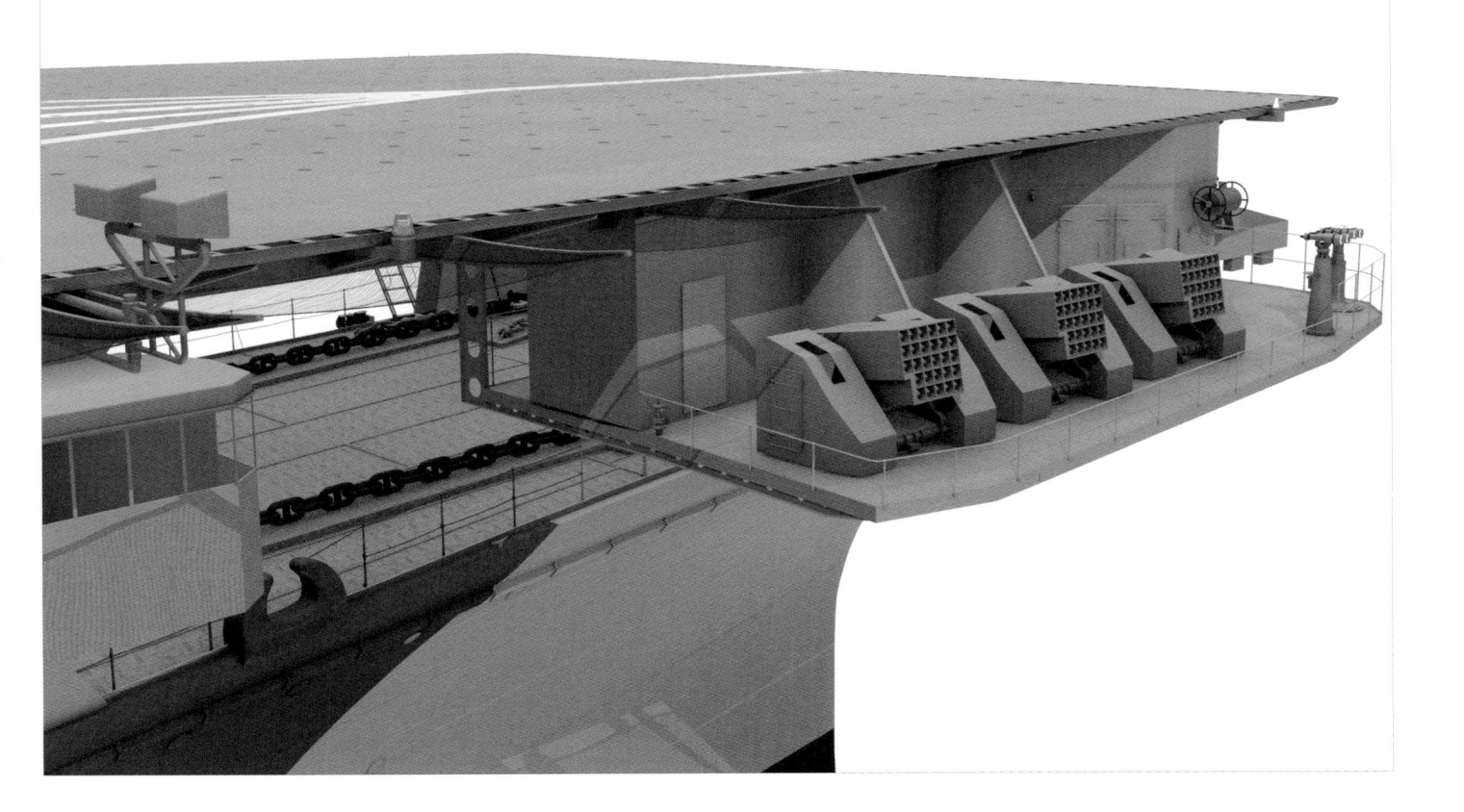

The Japanese Aircraft Carrier Shinano

Bow of *Shinano*.

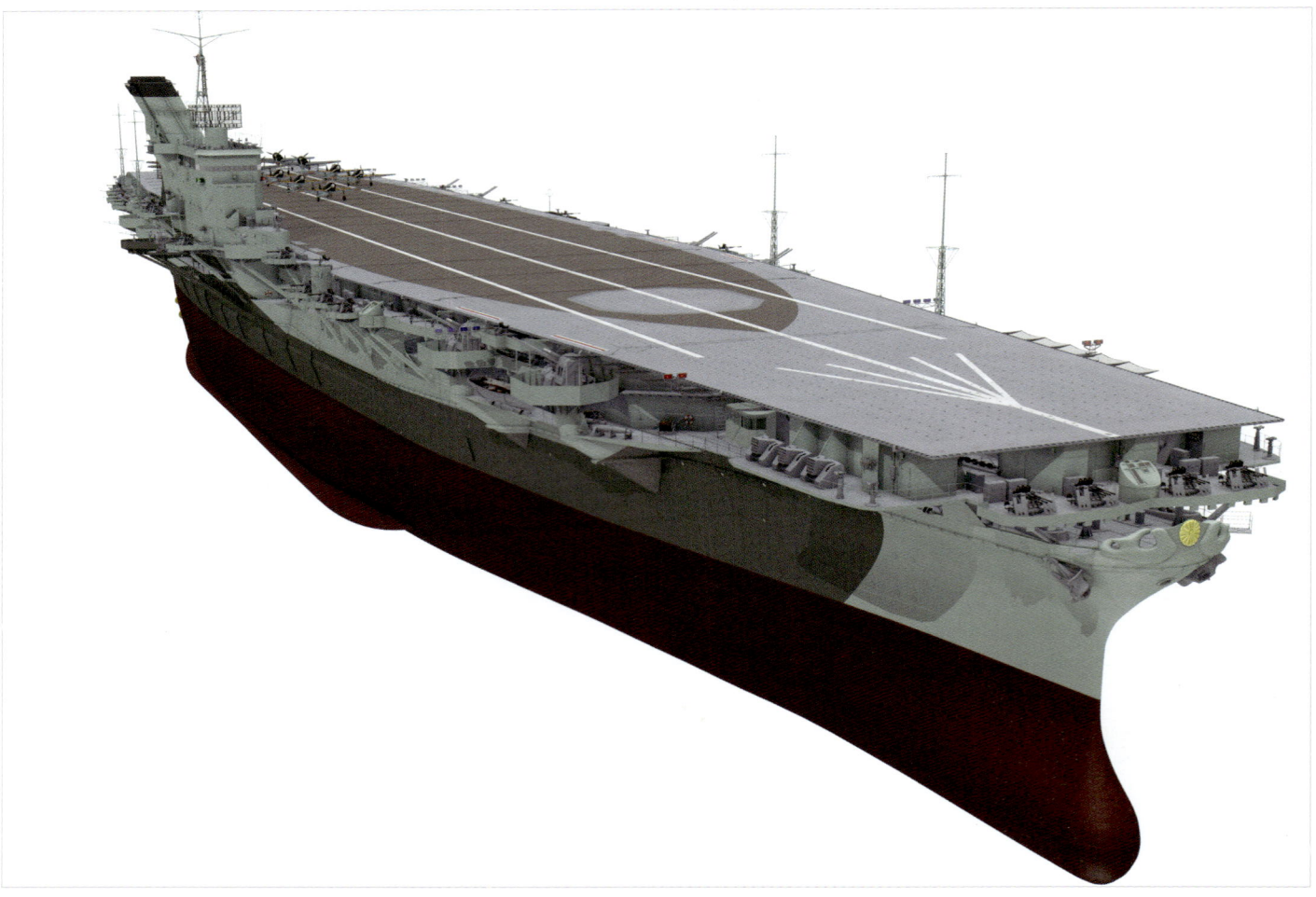

Superstructure and flight deck seen from the air.

The Japanese Aircraft Carrier Shinano

Rear view of *Shinano*.

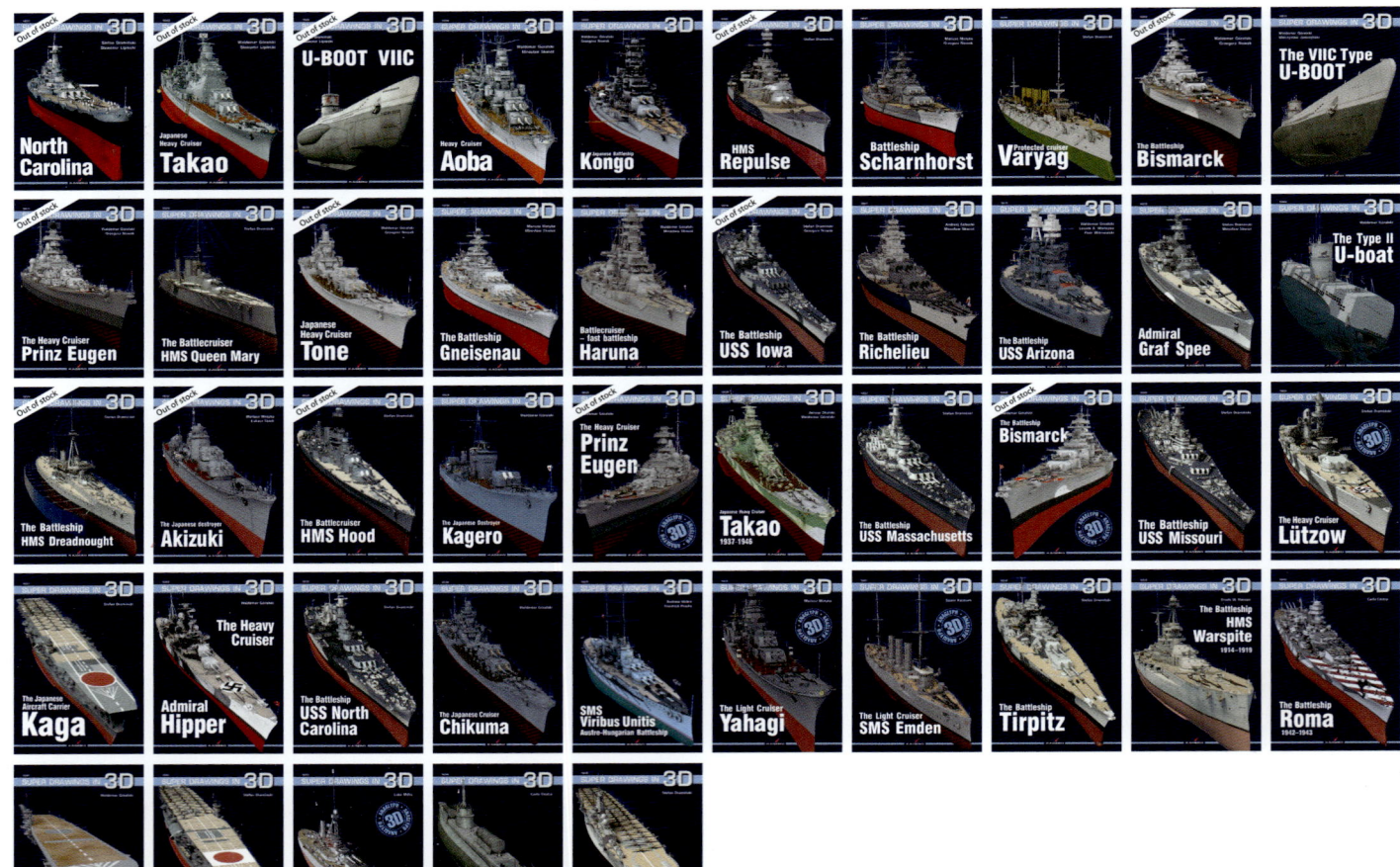

All available books on shop.kagero.pl

The Japanese Aircraft Carrier *Shinano* – Waldemar Góralski
LUBLIN 2016 • ISBN 978-83-65437-17-4
© All rights reserved. With the exception of quoting brief passages for the purposes of review, no part of this publication may be reproduced without prior written permission from the Publisher.
3D illustrations and captions: **Waldemar Góralski** • Text: **Piotr Wiśniewski** • Translation: **Jarosław Dobrzyński** • Design: **KAGERO STUDIO** – Marcin Wachowicz
KAGERO Publishing • www.kagero.pl, e-mail: kagero@kagero.pl, marketing@kagero.pl
Editorial office, Marketing, Distribution: KAGERO Publishing, Akacjowa 100, os. Borek, Turka, 20-258 Lublin 62, Poland, phone/fax (+48) 81 501 21 05
w w w . k a g e r o . e u